麦格希 中英双语阅读文库

# 人祸与天灾

【美】比林斯 (Billings, H.)　【美】比林斯 (Billings, M.) ●主编
赵罡●译
麦格希中英双语阅读文库编委会●编

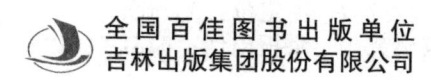

全国百佳图书出版单位
吉林出版集团股份有限公司

## 图书在版编目（CIP）数据

人祸与天灾 / (美) 比林斯 (Billings, H), (美) 比林斯 (Billings, M) 主编；赵罡译；麦格希中英双语阅读文库编委会编. -- 2版. -- 长春：吉林出版集团股份有限公司, 2018.3（2022.1重印）
（麦格希中英双语阅读文库）
ISBN 978-7-5581-4727-2

Ⅰ. ①人… Ⅱ. ①比… ②比… ③赵… ④麦… Ⅲ. ①英语—汉语—对照读物②灾害—青少年读物 Ⅳ. ①H319.4：X

中国版本图书馆CIP数据核字(2018)第046062号

### 人祸与天灾

| | |
|---|---|
| 编 | 麦格希中英双语阅读文库编委会 |
| 插　画 | 齐　航　李延霞 |
| 责任编辑 | 朱　玲 |
| 封面设计 | 冯冯翼 |
| 开　本 | 660mm × 960mm　1/16 |
| 字　数 | 214千字 |
| 印　张 | 9.5 |
| 版　次 | 2018年3月第2版 |
| 印　次 | 2022年1月第2次印刷 |
| 出　版 | 吉林出版集团股份有限公司 |
| 发　行 | 吉林出版集团外语教育有限公司 |
| 地　址 | 长春市福祉大路5788号龙腾国际大厦B座7层 |
| | 邮编：130011 |
| 电　话 | 总编办：0431-81629929 |
| | 发行部：0431-81629927　0431-81629921(Fax) |
| 印　刷 | 北京一鑫印务有限责任公司 |

ISBN 978-7-5581-4727-2　　　定价：35.00元
版权所有　　侵权必究　　举报电话：0431-81629929

# 前言 PREFACE

　　英国思想家培根说过：阅读使人深刻。阅读的真正目的是获取信息，开拓视野和陶冶情操。从语言学习的角度来说，学习语言若没有大量阅读就如隔靴搔痒，因为阅读中的语言是最丰富、最灵活、最具表现力、最符合生活情景的，同时读物中的情节、故事引人入胜，进而能充分调动读者的阅读兴趣，培养读者的文学修养，至此，语言的学习水到渠成。

　　"麦格希中英双语阅读文库"在世界范围内选材，涉及科普、社会文化、文学名著、传奇故事、成长励志等多个系列，充分满足英语学习者课外阅读之所需，在阅读中学习英语、提高能力。

　　◎难度适中

　　本套图书充分照顾读者的英语学习阶段和水平，从读者的阅读兴趣出发，以难易适中的英语语言为立足点，选材精心、编排合理。

◎精品荟萃

本套图书注重经典阅读与实用阅读并举。既包含国内外脍炙人口、耳熟能详的美文，又包含科普、人文、故事、励志类等多学科的精彩文章。

◎功能实用

本套图书充分体现了双语阅读的功能和优势，充分考虑到读者课外阅读的方便，超出核心词表的词汇均出现在使其意义明显的语境之中，并标注释义。

鉴于编者水平有限，凡不周之处，谬误之处，皆欢迎批评教正。

我们真心地希望本套图书承载的文化知识和英语阅读的策略对提高读者的英语著作欣赏水平和英语运用能力有所裨益。

丛书编委会

# Contents

## Smoke, Fire, and Death
浓烟烈火 / 1

### An Unexpected Explosion
意外爆炸 / 6

### The Fall of Saigon
西贡之战 / 14

### Firetrap!
易燃地带 / 22

### A Deadly Plunge
致命陷阱 / 30

### Nightmare in the Twin Towers
世贸噩梦 / 38

### Stay Out of the Water!
严禁下水 / 46

## A Sniper in the Tower
塔楼枪手 / 55

The Night the Dam Let Go
大坝崩塌 / 64

Flood in Mozambique
莫桑比克洪灾 / 73

Tragedy in the Baltic Sea
波罗的海悲歌 / 80

A Horrible Way to Die
恐怖死亡路 / 88

A Strangler Among Us
身边的谋杀犯 / 96

The Richard Riot
理查德骚乱 / 105

A Volcano Wakes Up
苏醒的火山 / 114

Death Rides the Subway
地铁死亡之旅 / 122

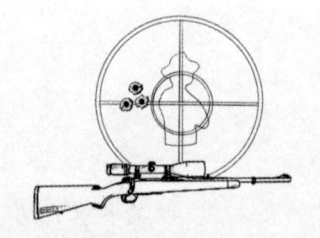

Hit by a Bullet
被子弹击中 / 130

Trapped on the 37th Floor
高楼遇困 / 138

# 1

# Smoke, Fire, and Death

"Fire! Fire!"

The cries *echoed* through the hallways of the 26-story hotel in Las Vegas, Nevada. On the 24th floor, Donald and Janet Tebbutt leaped out of bed. Donald pulled back the *drapes* and looked out the hotel window. All he could see was thick smoke billowing up from below. Frightened,

*A kitchen fire at Las Vegas's MGM Grand Hotel went out of control on the morning of November 21, 1980, causing fear and panic among the hotel's 4,500 guests.*

## 浓烟烈火

1980年11月21日清晨,拉斯维加斯MGM大酒店的厨房发生火灾,火势最终失控。这场大火引发了酒店里4500人的恐慌。

"着火了!着火了!"

惊呼声回荡在内华达州拉斯维加斯一栋26层楼酒店的走廊里。在24楼的一个房间里,唐纳德和他的妻子珍妮特·特巴特从床上一跃而起。唐纳德拉起窗帘,向酒店外望去,满目所见的全都是从楼下滚滚而上的浓

echo  *v.*  回响              drape  *n.*  (厚长的)帘子

## TOTAL PANIC

he and his wife ran out into the hallway. There, they met *swarms* of other guests. All were looking for the best way out. No one knew whether to go down the stairs or up to the roof. It was a scene of utter chaos.

The Tebbutts tried to make their way down the stairs. But the smoke in the *stairway* was simply too heavy. Turning around, they headed up toward the roof. But the stairway was becoming jammed with people. And the fumes and smoke were making it harder and harder to breathe.

As it turned out, the door to the roof was locked. There were windows, but they were lined with steel mesh and unbreakable. For a minute, it looked as though everyone in the stairwell was trapped. Then a man threw himself at the door. It popped open. People poured out onto the roof, gulping in fresh air.

All this happened on November 21, 1980. About 7:00 A.M. a

---

烟。他和妻子非常惊恐，冲到走廊里。在走廊里，他们遇到了蜂拥而至的其他客人。所有人都在寻找最快的逃生路线，没有人知道是应该下楼还是应该跑到楼顶上去，现场一片混乱。

唐纳德夫妇试图下楼，但楼道里全是滚滚的浓烟。他们转身往楼顶走，但是楼梯里已经堵满了人。浓烈的烟雾使人的呼吸变得越来越困难。

人们发现，通向楼顶的门是锁着的。虽然有窗户，但是这些窗户被钢丝网拦住，牢不可破。刹那间，好像楼道里的所有人都被困住了。这时，有个人向楼顶的这扇门撞去，门被撞开了。人们涌上楼顶，猛吸着新鲜空气。

所有这一切发生于1980年11月21日。大约在早上7点钟，拉斯维加斯

---

swarm *n.* 一大群 　　　　　　　　　　　　　　stairway *n.* 楼梯

◆ SMOKE, FIRE, AND DEATH

kitchen fire broke out in the MGM Grand Hotel in Las Vegas. The flames melted the alarm control box. Because of that, no alarm ever rang. The fire caught all 4,500 guests by surprise. There were other problems as well. None of the guest rooms had smoke detectors. And only the basement, first floor, and top floor had water *sprinklers*. "More sprinklers would have made all the difference in the world," a firefighter later said.

Police and fire trucks rushed to the scene. But the tallest rescue ladder reached only to the ninth floor. Everyone higher up was stranded. Many people climbed out onto their balconies. The police urged them to stay calm. Using *bullhorns*, police shouted, "Don't jump! Don't jump! The fire is under control!"

But one woman couldn't wait. She tied bedsheets together to make a rope. Then she crawled out her 19th floor window and headed down on the *makeshift* rope. She made it to the 17th floor.

---

MGM大酒店的厨房突然起火。大火烧毁了警报控制箱，所以警报器一直没有响。大火出其不意，袭击了共4500名客人。其他方面也存在问题。所有客房都没有烟雾探测器，只在地下室、一层和顶层里才装备有灭火器。一位消防队员事后说道："如果有更多的灭火器，情况就截然不同了。"

警察和消防车冲进事发现场。但是最高的救生云梯也只能伸到九楼，更高楼层里的人束手无策。很多人爬到阳台外边。警察劝他们保持冷静。警察对着扩音器高喊："不要往下跳！不要往下跳！火情已被控制！"

但是有位妇人等不下去了。她把床单系在一起做成一条绳子，然后她爬出19楼的窗户并沿着这根临时编结成的绳子往下爬。她爬到了17楼。

---

sprinkler *n.* （建筑物内的）自动喷水灭火装置　　　bullhorn *n.* 扩音器
makeshift *adj.* 临时的

**TOTAL PANIC**

Then she lost her grip and fell to her death.

Meanwhile, some guests were trapped in the halls. Many were overcome by the smoke. They slumped against walls, gasping for breath. Some people stayed in their rooms. A few wisely *soaked* towels and used them to block the smoke from seeping under the doors. "If they had stayed in their rooms until we got them," said Fire Chief Ralph Dinsman, "a lot of the dead would have survived."

About 200 people made it to the roof. Rescue helicopters *swooped* down to get them. But the helicopters could take only a few people at a time. Everyone wanted to be the first to leave. People started pushing and shoving. Luckily, someone in the crowd was a police officer. He pulled out his gun and yelled, "Stand back and keep cool or I will shoot." It worked. Everyone stepped back to wait his or her turn. Before long, all the people on the roof were rescued.

---

结果，她手没抓住，掉下来摔死了。

　　此时，有一些客人被困在走廊里，许多客人都被浓烟熏倒。他们跌坐在墙角，艰难地呼吸着。还有一些人停留在自己的房间里。很多人非常聪明，他们弄湿了毛巾，然后用湿毛巾堵住了从房门下面透进来的烟尘。消防队长拉尔夫·丁斯曼说道："如果他们坚持留在房间里，等着我们去救援，很多死者就能够幸存下来。"

　　大约有二百人跑到了楼顶。救援直升机降落到他们面前，但是直升机一次只能装下几个人。每个人都想最先离开这里。人们开始推推搡搡，幸亏人群中有一个警员，他拔出手枪高喊："都给我往后站，保持冷静，否则我就开枪了！"这句话起了作用。人们都往后退，等待轮到自己上直升机。不久，楼顶上所有人都得救了。

---

soak  *v.* 浸湿　　　　　　　　　　　swoop  *v.* 向下猛冲；俯冲

◆ SMOKE, FIRE, AND DEATH

Others were not so lucky. When the fire broke out, some gamblers didn't want to leave the first floor *casino*. They wanted to roll the dice or deal the cards one more time. The employees insisted on leaving. But 10 people stayed behind to *scoop up* their money and chips. All 10 died in the flames.

It wasn't the fire, however, that killed the most people. It was the smoke. The flames never got beyond the second floor. But black smoke funneled up the stairways to all 26 floors. Some people died in bed. One couple was found lying arm in arm. A waiter who had come to serve them breakfast lay dead on the floor beside them. In all, more than 700 people were injured and 84 people died. Kevin Beverton was one who made it out alive. When asked about the fire, he described it this way: "It was death, *absolute* death there."

---

其他人就不这么走运了。火灾发生时，有些赌徒不愿意离开第一层的赌场，他们想再掷一次骰子或者再玩一次纸牌。店员坚持让他们离开，可还是有10个人想留在后面收走他们的钱和筹码，结果这10个人全部在火灾中丧生。

不过，夺去大多数人生命的并不是大火。罪魁祸首是烟雾。大火从来没有燃烧到二楼以上，但是滚滚黑烟顺着楼道向上，充满了全部的26层楼。许多人死在床上。在现场，人们发现有一对夫妇相拥而死。一个来给他们送早餐的侍者倒在他们旁边的地板上，也死了。总共有七百多人受伤，84人丧生。凯文·毕佛特是幸存者之一。问及这场火灾时，他这样描述到："死亡之地，那里绝对是死亡之地。"

---

casino *n.* 赌场　　　　　　　　　　　　scoop up 拿起；拣起
absolute *adj.* 完全的；绝对的

## TOTAL PANIC

# 2

# An Unexpected Explosion

Most people in Edison, New Jersey, did not even know it was there. And why should they? The natural gas *pipeline* made no noise. It couldn't be seen. It was buried seven feet underground. For 33 years, this pipeline had done its job silently and without *incident*. It carried gas from Texas to the Northeast. Ten million

*After a nearby pipeline exploded, the terrific blast woke residents and sent them running for their lives.*

---

## 意外爆炸

附近的输气管道爆炸后，可怕的爆炸惊醒了居民，人们奔走逃命。

新泽西州艾迪逊市的大多数人根本不知道他们的天然气管道铺设在哪里。而且，他们为什么要知道这个事儿呢？天然气管道不会发出声响，也根本看不见。管道铺设在7英尺深的地下。33年来，它们安静地工作着，从未出现过偏差。这些管道把天然气从德克萨斯输送到美国东北部，是一千万户

---

pipeline n. 管道        incident n. 严重事件

◆ AN UNEXPECTED EXPLOSION

homes got fuel from it. It was like a good neighbor—quiet and helpful.

But on March 23, 1994, the pipeline made its *presence* known in an awful way. At 11:58 P.M., it blew up. The blast occurred near the Durham Woods Apartments. More than 1,500 people lived there. The explosion was deafening. It blew a hole in the ground 120 feet wide and 60 feet deep. A huge tower of flames shot 400 feet into the air. It turned the sky a bright orange. The flames could be seen 30 miles away in New York City.

The people of Edison had no idea what had hit them. Was it a thunderstorm? A *tornado*? A rocket attack? "I thought it was the end of the world," said Barbara Barone.

She wasn't alone. Many other people thought the same thing.

---

家庭的燃气来源，它就像是一个好邻居——宁静安详，乐于助人。

但是，1994年3月23日，这管道以一种糟糕的方式让世人知道了它的存在。那天深夜11时58分，管道突然发生爆炸。爆炸点位于达拉谟森林公寓附近，那里居民超过1500人。爆炸声震耳欲聋。地面被炸出一个120英尺宽、60英尺深的大坑。巨大的火舌伸向空中，长达400英尺。天空被映照成亮桔红色。在30英里外的纽约城里都能看到这里的熊熊火焰。

艾迪逊市的人不知道什么东西在攻击他们，是突降雷暴雨？是刮龙卷风？还是火箭来袭？芭芭拉·巴隆说："我还以为世界末日到了呢！"

这种感觉并非她独有。很多人都是这样认为的。吉姆·克拉涅克说：

---

presence　n.　存在　　　　　　　　　　tornado　n.　龙卷风

**TOTAL PANIC**

Said Kim Krajniak, "My first thought was 'It's a nuclear bomb. We're dead.'" Terrence Reed called his father in nearby Piscataway to tell him that a nuclear bomb had been dropped.

The blast awakened everyone in the area. People jumped out of bed and ran for their lives. Many carried pets or babies under their arms. Some were so frightened that they didn't stop to put on clothes. Others grabbed coats or sweaters against the evening chill. As it turned out, they didn't need them. The heat from the *blaze* was a searing 1000°F. A few people took flashlights. But they didn't need those, either. The orange light was brighter than the noonday sun.

The *residents* of Durham Woods were scared out of their minds. "No words could ever tell you how frightening it was," said Kim Krajniak. "People were running out in their underwear. I felt like an

---

"我的第一感觉是原子弹爆炸了，大家都死了。"特雷斯·里德给住在附近皮斯卡塔维镇的父亲打电话，告诉父亲有颗原子弹掉落下来。

爆炸惊醒了这一地区的所有人。人们跳下床来，拔腿逃命。很多人带着宠物，腋下夹着孩子；有些人惊慌失措，甚至连衣服都没有穿上；有些人抓过外衣，套上毛衫，以此抵御深夜的风寒。事实证明，他们根本用不着这些东西。烈焰温度高达灼人的1000华氏度。一些人拿着手电筒，但拿这些东西也毫无意义，橙色的火光比正午的太阳还要亮。

达拉谟森林的居民们惊吓过度。吉姆·克拉涅克说："无法用言语形容事情有多么可怕，人们穿着内衣跑了出来，就像野兽在逃命一样。真是

---

blaze n. 烈火；火焰      resident n. 居民

◆ AN UNEXPECTED EXPLOSION

animal running scared for my life."

People ran in all directions. Some headed for their cars only to burn their hands on the door handles. Some ran into the woods. Others dashed down the nearby railroad tracks. Those who could run fast pushed slower runners out of the way. Some stepped on people who had *stumbled*. Marlene Steinberg said it was "mass *hysteria*." She ran like everyone else. "We didn't know where we were going," she said, "but we kept going."

Barbara Williams didn't pay any attention to where she was headed. "Nobody had to give me directions," she said. "All I wanted to do was to get out of there as fast as I possibly could. And let me tell you, I ran like there was no tomorrow."

The *blast* shook Joy Anunwa out of bed. For a brief moment the

---

一场噩梦!"

　　人们四散奔逃。有些人跑向他们的汽车，没想到被车门把手烫着了；有些人跑向森林；另一些人冲向附近的铁路。跑得快的人把跑得慢的人推到路边，很多人踩到摔倒的人身上。马琳·施坦博格称其为"集体狂乱"。她和其他人一样奔跑。她说道："我们不知道要跑向哪里，但我们仍然坚持奔跑。"

　　芭芭拉·威廉姆斯根本不在意自己跑向何方。她说："没有人指给我方向，我能做的就是尽快逃离那个地方。跟你说吧，我奔跑着，就好像时间没有下一刻。"

　　爆炸声把乔伊·安诺娃从床上惊醒。转瞬间，强光使她双眼什么都

---

stumble *v.* 跌倒；蹒跚　　　　　　hysteria *n.* 歇斯底里；情绪狂暴不可抑止
blast *n.* 爆炸

## TOTAL PANIC

light blinded her. Anunwa pinched herself. She wondered whether she had died and gone to heaven. Then she opened her apartment door. "The heat was like an oven... It was right out of a disaster movie." She and her family headed for the woods.

The *flames* near the apartments began to spread. The intense heat melted the tires of cars. It blew out car windows and *scorched* the paint. When it reached the playground, the heat melted the swing sets. Luckily, a 20-foot dirt *mound* separated the apartment buildings from the fire. The mound slowed the fire's spread. It gave people about 10 minutes to get out. Those 10 minutes saved many lives.

When the fire did reach the apartment *complex*, it burned eight buildings to the ground. It damaged six others. Toni Strauch of the Red Cross said it was like an earthquake. "One day people have

---

看不见了。安诺娃缩作一团。她想知道自己是否已经死了，进了天堂。然后，她打开房门。"热度跟烤炉似的……那就像灾难片一样。"她和家人跑向森林。

公寓附近的火势开始蔓延。强热使汽车轮胎熔化，火焰使车窗爆裂，汽车喷漆被烧焦。火势蔓延到操场上，秋千全被烧坏了。万幸的是，一个20英尺高的土堆把公寓建筑和大火隔离开来。土堆减缓了火势的蔓延，人们由此得到了10分钟的撤离时间。正是这10分钟救了许多人的命。

大火蔓延到公寓群，有8栋建筑被烧塌，另有6栋被烧坏。红十字会成员托妮·斯塔赫说现场就像经历了一场地震。她说道："人们原来什么

---

flame  *n.*  火焰  
mound  *n.*  土堆；土丘  
scorch  *v.*  （把……）烫坏，烧焦  
complex  *n.*  （类型相似的）建筑群

◆ AN UNEXPECTED EXPLOSION

everything," she said. "The next day they are *devastated*."

In time, firefighters brought the blaze under control. Still, they feared the worst. The fire had totally wiped out 128 apartments. How many people would be found dead inside? Edison's mayor expected the death toll to be high. He couldn't believe it when he heard the truth. Only one person had died. She was a 32-year-old woman who had suffered a heart attack. Many others were left with burns or injuries. But no one else *perished*. Incredibly, the fire itself didn't kill anyone. The mayor called it "a miracle of miracles."

Still, the terror didn't die out with the fire. "I try not to think about it," said Danielle Rhodes. But that was hard to do. The blast was imprinted on her mind. Four-year-old Michelle Varner also had trouble forgetting the explosion. In the nights that followed, she

---

都有，但现在，所有东西都毁于一旦了。"

消防队员及时控制住了火势。尽管如此，人们还是惊恐到了极点。大火烧掉了128栋公寓建筑，里面会有多少死者呢？艾迪逊市市长预计死亡人数会很高。确切数字报上来时，市长都不敢相信自己的耳朵：仅有一人丧生。死者是一位32岁的妇人，死因是突发心脏病。很多幸存者有的被烧伤，有的受了外伤。除那位妇人外，无人送命。难以置信，大火本身并没有导致任何人死亡。市长称这是"奇迹中的奇迹"。

但是人们的恐惧感并没有随着大火被扑灭而消失。丹妮尔·罗德说："我尽量不去想它。"但这一点却很难做到，爆炸留在她的记忆深处。4

---

devastate *v.* 彻底破坏；毁灭　　　　　　　　　　　perish *v.* 死亡

## TOTAL PANIC

couldn't sleep. When her mother put her to bed, the little girl cried, "Mommy, when is the boom coming? I don't want to go to bed, the *boom* is coming."

Michelle's eight-year-old brother, Paris, had the same fear. "I don't want to go back [to my house]," he said. "I just want to move somewhere else. They said the pipeline had a hole in it. But even if they fix that, it could have another hole." Many Durham Woods residents shared his feelings.

But it is not easy to move away from gas pipelines. With its many branches, this one runs a total of about 26 thousand miles. Many of us live near this or similar pipelines. We just have to be more careful. Officials think the *leak* at Edison was caused by digging. Someone used the ground near the pipeline as a dump. Officials found

---

岁大的米歇尔·瓦纳也忘不掉这次爆炸。接下来的一些晚上，她无法睡着。当妈妈把她放到床上时，这个小女孩哭喊道："妈妈，轰隆隆的声音什么时候来？我不想上床睡觉，轰隆隆的声音要来了。"

米歇尔8岁大的哥哥，帕里斯，也同样害怕。他说："我不想回去，我只想去别的什么地方。他们说管道上有个大洞。可就算他们修好了，别的地方也会有大洞的。"达拉谟森林的很多居民都和他有同感。

可是把天然气管道移开并不是很容易的事情。管道有众多分支，总长大约两万六千英里。很多人都生活在这里或与其类似的管道附近。人们只能更加小心翼翼。政府官员们认为艾迪逊市的管道泄漏是由挖掘工作引起

---

boom *n.* 隆隆声        leak *n.* 漏洞；裂缝

◆ AN UNEXPECTED EXPLOSION

55-gallon drums buried there. They found a crushed car buried on top of the pipeline. They also found car tires and steel rods buried there. In the process of burying these things, someone had dug into the ground. That could have weakened the pipe and caused the leak.

There are laws against such *random* digging. You can't just decide to dig a hole in the ground. All sorts of pipes and wires might be running below the ground. You don't know what you might hit. There are maps that show where the pipes and wires are. Clearly, someone in Edison didn't check. The result *scared* one person to death. And it left others with fears that won't go away.

---

的。有人把管道附近的地方当作废物堆放处。官员们在那里发现掩埋着的圆桶，总容积有55加仑。一辆被压碎的小汽车就横在管道上方。他们在那个地方还发现汽车轮胎和铁棍。在掩埋这些废物的过程中，一定有人挖掘到地底深处。这样就会损伤天然气管道并且导致其泄漏。

法律对这种随意挖掘明文禁止：一个人不能随便决定在某处地面进行挖掘活动。因为可能所有的管道和缆线都铺设在地下，个人单独进行地面挖掘时就不知道会碰到什么东西。有专门的地下管线走向图。但很显然，艾迪逊市的某个人并没有仔细查看它们，由此导致最终一人惊吓而死，并且，这起事故在其他人的心灵里留下了永恒的恐惧感。

---

random *adj.* 随意的；任意的　　　　　　　　　　scare *v.* 惊吓

## TOTAL PANIC

# 3

# The Fall of Saigon

Diem Do tried to be a good student. But it was hard. Each day he went to school. But each day his class got smaller. "One day a couple of guys would be gone, and then a couple more. Then the teacher wouldn't show up," said 12-year-old Do. "Everyone was scared. They *sensed* that something *tragic* was

*Under attack by North Vietnamese forces, terrified South Vietnamese hurry to reach U.S. helicopters as they prepare to pull out of Saigon.*

## 西贡之战

在北越军队的攻势下，惊恐的南越人匆匆登上美国的直升机。此情此景，仿佛他们要把西贡市全部带走。

戴姆·杜想成为一名好学生，但这的确很难。他每天都去上学，但他所在班级的规模每天都在缩小。12岁的杜说道："有一天，两个小孩要走。后来，有更多的孩子要走。然后，老师就不来了。每个人都很害怕。他们觉得有什么悲惨的事情就要发生了。"

---

sense  *v.*  察觉到；意识到              tragic  *adj.*  悲惨的

◆ THE FALL OF SAIGON

about to happen."

It was April 1975. Do was going to school in Saigon, then the *capital* of South Vietnam. That country had been fighting North Vietnam for many years. Now the war was almost over. The United States had fought on the side of South Vietnam. But it was no use. A big army from North Vietnam was *marching* south. Its goal was to take over Saigon and end the war.

The Americans had gotten ready for the worst. They had plans to get themselves out of Saigon when the time came. By this time there weren't many Americans still there. Most had left years before. The problem was what to do with America's South Vietnamese friends. These people, too, hoped to get out before the enemy arrived. But there were far too many South Vietnamese. U.S. planes began to fly a few people out. But this was done slowly and quietly. Officials feared

---

1975年4月，杜要上学了，就在西贡，后来的南越首都。南越和北越连年争战。此时，战事已近尾声。美国支持南越一方，但也无济于事。庞大的北越军队正开往南方。这支军队的目的就是控制西贡，结束战争。

美国人已经作了最坏的准备。他们已经筹划适时撤离西贡。此时已经没有太多美国人留在那里，大多数人前些年就离开了。现在的问题是如何对待美国的南越盟友，这些人也希望在敌军到来前撤离此地。但南越人实在是太多了。美国飞机开始将一部分人空运出来，但这项工作只能缓慢而

---

capital  n.  首都                                             march  v.  行军

## TOTAL PANIC

that if too many people thought the end was close, they might *panic*.

The army from the North, meanwhile, had its own *schedule*, and it was moving fast. By the last week of April, the army had Saigon surrounded. Each night, a college student named Nam Pham climbed to the roof of his home. He could see flashes of gunfire and bombs in the far distance. They kept getting closer and closer. Pham knew the South would soon lose. "It gave me kind of a *weird* feeling," he said, "watching something you love so much lost a little bit every day."

On April 29, the North attacked Saigon itself. At four o'clock in the morning, they began to bomb the airport. When the Americans turned on their radios that morning, they heard "White Christmas." That song was a secret signal. It meant, "This is it. Everybody out!"

For the Vietnamese it was a different story. The blasts at the

---

安静地进行。长官们担心，如果末日将至的想法笼罩在太多人的心头，就可能引发大面积的恐慌。

此时，北越的部队已经制定了行军表，并快速地行进着。到了四月的最后一个星期，北越军队已包围西贡。每天晚上，大学生纳姆·费姆都会爬到他家的屋顶上。他能看到远处的炮火和炸弹的闪光。火光越来越近了，费姆知道南方很快就要战败了。他说："亲眼看着自己所热爱的东西每天一点点地丢失，这给了我一种奇异的感觉。"

4月29日，北越军攻陷西贡。凌晨4点，北越军队开始轰炸机场。清晨，当美国人打开收音机时，他们听到的是"白色圣诞歌"。这是一个暗号，意味着："一切都结束了，所有人都离开了。"

对越南人来说，事情就不同了。机场传来的爆炸声惊醒了每一个

---

panic *v.* 恐慌        schedule *n.* 日程安排

weird *adj.* 奇异的；古怪的

◆ THE FALL OF SAIGON

airport shook them out of their beds. Mass panic *gripped* the city. People dashed out of their homes, looking for a way—any way—to get out of town. Some people boarded boats and headed out to sea. The U.S. Navy had many large ships waiting *offshore*.

Loi Nguyen Vo was one of the lucky ones. She was living with her mother and six younger *siblings*. "We had to leave quickly with only the clothes on our back," she said. Taking charge, Vo went to look for a boat. Thousands of others lined the riverbank oping for the same thing. Out of the mist, a patrol boat came by and picked up Vo and her family. "I still don't know why we were picked. We were very lucky," said Vo many years later.

Many Vietnamese rushed to the U.S. *embassy*. The Americans had been their friends. Surely America would help them now. But what could the Americans do? There were thousands of people

---

人。巨大的恐慌情绪笼罩在城市上空。人们冲到屋外，寻找逃离城市的方法———一切方法。有些人登上小船，逃往海上。海面上，美国海军的多艘大型船舶在等待着他们。

罗伊·恩吉耶·沃是幸运儿之一。她和妈妈、6个弟弟妹妹住在一起。她说："我们不得不背着衣物，仓促离开。"沃拿着零钱，出去寻找小船。数千人怀着同样的想法，排在河岸边。一艘巡逻艇穿过白雾，开到近前，让沃这一家人上去。多年以后，沃说："我还是不知道他们为什么会让我们上去，我们真走运。"

很多越南人冲进美国大使馆。美国人是他们的朋友，现在美国人当然会帮助他们，但美国人又能做些什么呢？成千上万人挤在大使馆门前，他

---

grip *v.* 对……产生强有力的影响
sibling *n.* 兄；弟；姐；妹

offshore *adv.* 近海地
embassy *n.* 大使馆

## TOTAL PANIC

swarming around the embassy gates. They all wanted to flee. But time was running out. The North was closing in. Frank Snepp, an American, tried to *restore* order. "Don't worry," he told the mob. "We won't leave you!" Snepp was lying. There was no way to *evacuate* this many people in just a few hours. He later said the scene was like a "vision out of a *nightmare*."

The bombing closed the airport. So no one could fly out from there. Driving out of town wasn't possible either. The army of the North had all the roads blocked. Other than by boat, the only way out was by helicopter. American pilots flew helicopters *back and forth* from the ships at sea to Saigon. They had to land on the roof of the embassy. It was the only safe flat place they could find. The pilots took as many Vietnamese as they could. But far more had to be left behind. "These people were desperate to escape," said one pilot.

---

们都想逃走。但是时间所剩无几，北越军队已经逼近。一个美国人，弗兰克·斯奈普，试图使秩序恢复原样。他冲着人群说道："不要担心，我们不会扔下你们不管的！"他在说谎，根本没有办法在仅有的几小时内让这么多人安全撤离。后来，他形容当时的景象就像是一场"超级噩梦"。

　　北越军的轰炸已经离机场很近了，因此没有飞机能从那里起飞。也不可能用车辆把人们运出城，北越军队已经封锁了所有公路。除了小船，唯有的逃生办法就是乘直升机。美军飞行员驾驶直升机往返于海面上的船舶与西贡之间。直升机不得不降落在大使馆楼顶，这是他们找到仅有的一块安全之地。飞行员让尽可能多的越南人登机，但更多的人只能留在后面。一位飞行员说："人们不顾一切想要逃走，但我们只能救上来这么多

---

restore *v.* 恢复
nightmare *n.* 噩梦

evacuate *v.* 撤离
back and forth 来回地

◆ THE FALL OF SAIGON

"But we could only hold so many."

Tini Tran was only three years old at the time. Many years later she could still recall what it was like. Her parents brought her to the embassy gates. But they soon lost her in the crowd. Luckily Tran's uncle found her. "He *hoisted* me up as he shoved his way through the crowd," recalled Tran. "Afraid I would become *trampled* in the crush, my uncle handed me into the arms of an American." Luckily the rest of her family also made it out.

If the fall of Saigon had any heroes, they were the helicopter pilots. Time after time they risked their lives. Darrell Browning had never flown in *combat*. Now he faced many dangers. He worried about being shot down. The army of the North could do it. So, too, could a soldier from the South. Some of these soldiers were angry at the United States for leaving them alone to face the enemy. Also,

---

人。"

　　提尼·川恩当时只有3岁。多年以后她仍然能够回忆起当时的情况。父母抱着她来到大使馆门前，但很快，在人群中，他们就把她弄丢了。幸好川恩的叔叔找到了她。川恩回忆道："他把我举起来，这样他才能够在人群中穿行。我叔叔怕我被踩着，就把我送到了一个美国人的臂弯里。"幸运的是川恩的其他家人也挤出了人群。

　　如果说在这个西贡之战里有英雄的话，非直升机飞行员莫属。每次营救，他们都冒着生命危险。达雷尔·伯朗宁从未执行过战斗飞行任务。现在，他面临诸多危险。他担心被击落，北越军队里很多人都能做到这一点。当然，南越士兵也可能这么干。因为有些南越士兵对美国人撇下他

---

hoist　v.　吊起；拉高　　　　　　　　trample　v.　踩伤；踩踏
combat　n.　打仗；战斗

**TOTAL PANIC**

Browning flew late into the night with his lights out. With *choppers* flying all over the place, he might have hit one in *midair*. Luckily, nothing like that happened.

Each time Browning landed on the roof, people fought each other for a seat. He helped as many as he could. His chopper was built to carry 24 people. Still, he let 36 get on board. He figured the Vietnamese people tended to be small, so they weighed less. Even so, he worried he couldn't take off with all the extra weight. Somehow, he did. By midnight, he had made five round trips between his ship and the roof.

Then he was told to stop. It was over. The chopper pilots were worn out. One *exhausted* pilot missed his ship and *crashed* into the sea. The officer in charge worried that other pilots would also make tragic mistakes.

---

们，让他们独自对付敌军感到愤怒。伯朗宁也是深夜出航，没有开航灯。在整个航程中，他很可能撞到半空中的什么东西，但他很幸运，类似的情况并没有发生。

　　每当伯朗宁把直升机降落在屋顶上，人们都会为争夺一个座位而相互厮打。他竭尽所能，帮助他们。直升机额定载荷24人。尽管如此，伯朗宁还是让36人登机。他认为，越南人体型较小，因此体重很轻。尽管如此，他还是不敢保证超载之后可以起飞。不管怎么样，他还是这样做了。午夜时分，他在船舶与屋顶之间往返了五次。

　　随即他被叫停。不能再这样做了。直升机飞行员们都疲劳过度。曾有一名精疲力竭的飞行员因找不到所属的船舶，而坠入大海。长官担心其他飞行员可能也会犯这种悲惨的错误。

---

chopper　*n.*　直升机  
exhausted　*adj.*　精疲力竭的；疲惫不堪的  

midair　*n.*　半空中  
crash　*v.*　撞击；猛撞

◆ THE FALL OF SAIGON

The next day, April 30, the army of the North *captured* Saigon. The war was over. In all, about 50,000 South Vietnamese escaped. Some were on the *deck* of Darrell Browning's ship. Many were the people he had helped to save the night before. "There were about a thousand of them," he said. "They had lost everything. They had no idea where they were going and they were tired. But they were orderly and thankful. They came up and thanked us." For them, at least, the nightmare was over.

---

第二天，4月30日，北越军队占领西贡，战争结束了。共有5万南越人逃往国外。一些人挤在达雷尔·伯朗宁所在船的甲板上，其中有很多人是他前一天晚上营救出来的。他说："大概有一千人，他们一无所有，不知要去向何方。他们非常疲倦。但他们很有秩序，并且心存感激。他们走过来向我们道谢。"至少，对于那些人来说，噩梦结束了。

---

capture  v.  占领；夺取　　　　　　　　　　　　deck  n.  甲板

TOTAL PANIC

# 4

# Firetrap!

Julio Gonzalez was mad—really mad. First, he had lost his job. Now he was broke. He had to *hustle* spare change from strangers on the streets of New York City. And to top it all off, his girlfriend, Lydia Feliciano, had just said she did not want to see him *anymore*.

*The Happy Land Club did not live up to its name in the early morning hours of March 25, 1990. The tiny club had been filled with fun-seekers, mostly Honduran immigrants. All but five of the 92 people inside died in a fire set by the angry boyfriend of a club employee.*

## 易燃地带

1990年3月25日早上的这段时间，欢乐谷夜总会并不像它的名字那样快乐。这个微型的夜总会里挤满了寻欢作乐的人，其中绝大多数是洪都拉斯移民。92人中，大多数死于一场火灾，只有5人幸免于难。这场火灾由一个夜总会店员的男朋友一时愤怒而引起。

朱力奥·冈萨雷斯疯了——真的疯了。他先是失去了工作，现在已经伤透了心，所以不得不到纽约街头抢陌生人的零钱。最糟糕的是，他的女朋友，丽达·菲利西诺刚刚对他说，永远都不想再见到他了。

hustle v. （常指非法地）取得；强行　　　　anymore adv. （不）再

◆ FIRETRAP!

Gonzalez hoped to win Lydia back. On March 24, 1990, he went to see her at the Happy Land Club in the Bronx. Lydia worked there taking tickets and checking coats. But things didn't go the way Gonzalez had planned. The two began to argue. "Leave me alone! Leave me alone!" Lydia cried.

Gonzalez, who had been drinking, wasn't thinking clearly. He became *furious*. He started swearing at her. At that point, the club *bouncer* told him to leave. "I will be back," Gonzalez threatened. "I will shut this place down."

Gonzalez kept his dire threat. Around three o'clock the next morning, he returned to the club. He carried with him a *plastic* can filled with *gasoline*. He had paid a dollar for it at a local gas station. Gonzalez splashed the gasoline around the club's front door. Then

冈萨雷斯想赢回丽达的芳心。1990年3月24日，他去布朗克斯的欢乐谷夜总会见她。丽达在那里售票，看管衣物。但事情没有像冈萨雷斯预想的那样发展。两个人开始争吵。丽达大喊："走开！离我远点儿！"

冈萨雷斯喝了很多酒，已经神志不清了。他变得疯狂起来，开始诅咒丽达。此时，夜总会里的保镖让他离开。冈萨雷斯恐吓道："我会回来的，我会让你们破产的！"

冈萨雷斯履行了他那可怕的誓言。第二天凌晨，大概三点钟，他返回这家夜总会。他随身带着一个塑料罐，里面装满了汽油。这是他在当地一个加油站花一美元买来的。冈萨雷斯把汽油泼在夜总会门口，点着一根火

furious *adj.* 狂怒的
plastic *adj.* 塑料的

bouncer *n.* 保镖
gasoline *n.* 汽油

**TOTAL PANIC**

he *tossed* a lighted match on the gas. As the flames climbed up the door, Gonzalez just stood there and watched. Then he walked down the street and back to his room.

Inside the club were dozens of young people. Most were *immigrants* from Honduras. They had packed the place, coming to dance and have a good time. They were listening to the music they loved—salsa, reggae, and calypso. One lucky man had left at one o'clock. The club was too crowded for him. "You could barely move," he later said. "I had a feeling something could go wrong."

Even without Julio Gonzalez, there were lots of things that could have gone wrong at Happy Land. The club was unsafe. The city had ordered it closed 16 months earlier. The small, two-story club was a *firetrap*. It had no fire exits or emergency lights. It had no sprinkler

柴，扔在上面。大火烧到门口，冈萨雷斯就站在那里看着，然后他沿着大街走回自己家中。

此时夜总会里有许多年轻人，其中绝大多数是洪都拉斯移民。他们拥在这里，尽情地跳舞，非常快乐。他们听着喜爱的音乐——赛尔斯、瑞格舞曲、卡里普索。有个人一点钟离开了那里，他很走运。对他来说，夜总会里实在太拥挤了。晚些时候，他说："几乎挪不动步，我觉得有什么事情出了问题。"

即使没有朱力奥·冈萨雷斯，欢乐谷里也会出很多问题。这家夜总会并不安全。16个月以前，市政当局就勒令这里停业。这个小型的，有着二层楼的夜总会很容易失火。这里没有安全出口和应急灯，没有安装消防系

toss  v. 扔；投  　　　　　　　　　　　immigrant  n. 移民
firetrap  n. 易引起火灾的建筑物

◆ FIRETRAP!

system. It didn't have a fire alarm.

Lots of people knew about the fire *hazards*. A man named Jerome Ford explained how he had tried to warn his family. He had spoken to his niece, his cousin, and his wife's three brothers. "I told them not to go," he said. "But kids are kids. I knew it was dangerous."

The dangers meant nothing to Elias Colon, the club's owner. To him, the Happy Land Club was a great moneymaker. So he kept the place open. Although the city had told him to close it, officials did nothing to *enforce* the order. One city worker explained how hard it was to get such places closed down. "You shut them down one day, and they reopen the next," he said.

New York City had hundreds of these clubs. They were all *illegal*. None had the city *licenses* they needed. Few, if any, met the city's fire

---

统，也没有火灾警报器。

很多人知道那里存在火灾隐患。一个叫杰罗姆·福特的男人说他曾经警告过家人。他告诉侄女、堂兄妹和他妻子的3个弟弟，让他们别去那儿，但他们不太听话。他说："我知道那里很危险。"

但对这家夜总会的老板伊莱亚斯·科隆来说，这些隐患根本不算什么。对他来说，欢乐谷夜总会就是一台巨大的赚钱机器，因此他坚持照常营业。尽管市政当局让他关门，但官员们并没有强制执行。一名上班族解释了关掉这样一个地方有多么困难的原因，他说："头一天你让他们关门，第二天他们又开始营业了。"

纽约城里有几百家这样的夜总会，全是非法经营的。它们都没有营业执照，仅有少数加入了城市火灾预警系统。但是这些"社交俱乐部"似

---

hazard *n.* 危险  
illegal *adj.* 非法的

enforce *v.* 实施；执行  
license *n.* 批准；许可

**TOTAL PANIC**

code. But these "social clubs" seemed to fill a void in people's lives. They gave immigrants a place to relax with their own people. They were an old tradition in New York City.

The Happy Land Club was not an *exception*. Most of the regulars were looking for a club of their own. They had settled on Happy Land. The prices were low, and the music was loud. It even felt a bit like home. "It was great," said one man. "You could dance, you could get a drink. It was beautiful."

But there was nothing beautiful about it in the early morning of March 25, 1990. The blaze Gonzalez had set spread quickly. Thick black smoke *billowed* up inside the club. It soon reached the second-story dance floor, where all the people were. Not only did this area lack fire exits, it also lacked windows. The people up here were

---

乎可以填补人们日常生活中的空虚。它们给移民提供了一个放松身心的场所，并且在纽约城已经存在很久了。

欢乐谷夜总会也不例外。多数常住人口都会选定一家俱乐部，并经常光顾。他们选中了欢乐谷。这里价格低廉，音乐狂放有力，甚至给人一种家的感觉。一个客人说："这里非常好，你可以跳舞，可以喝酒，太美妙了！"

但是在1990年3月25日早上，一切都黯然失色。冈萨雷斯引燃的大火迅速蔓延开来。滚滚黑烟在夜总会里翻腾，很快燃烧到二楼的舞厅。所有人都聚在那里。这里不仅缺少安全出口，也缺少窗户。人们被困在里面。有些人跑到楼梯口，想下到一楼去，但其中大多数被火焰所阻。只有少数

---

exception *n.* 例外          billow *v.* （烟雾）涌出；大量冒出

trapped. Some ran to the stairs, hoping to get down to the first floor. But the fire stopped most of them. A few did make it down. But even then, there was no way out. There were two small windows on the ground floor. But both were blocked. One had bars, and the other held an *air conditioner*.

Firefighters got to the scene as fast as they could. They heard no screams. They saw no one fleeing from the building. The people trapped inside were already dead. Sixty-eight bodies were found on the second floor. Nineteen more were discovered on the ground level. Among the dead was Happy Land owner Elias Colon.

It was the smoke, not the fire, that killed most people. The smoke *suffocated* them before they could react. Some died so fast they still had their drinks in their hands; some still had their legs wrapped

人跑下楼，但他们仍然无路可逃。一楼有两扇小窗户，但是都无法打开。一扇窗上有许多栅栏，另一扇窗前放着一台空调。

消防队员以最快的速度冲到现场。他们没有听到呼救声，没有看见一个人从那栋建筑中逃出。被困在里面的人已经全部遇难。人们在二楼发现了68具尸体，在一楼又发现另外19具。死者中就有欢乐谷夜总会的老板伊莱亚斯·科隆。

导致大多数人死亡的原因是浓烟，而不是大火。人们还没来得及做出反应，浓烟就已经让他们窒息而亡。有些人很快就死掉了，酒水还在手里端着；有些人还跨坐在凳子上；很多人躲到墙角，企盼浓烟不会跑那么远。

air conditioner 空调　　　　　　　　　　suffocate *v.* 使窒息

### TOTAL PANIC

around a bar stool. Many had thrown themselves into corners, hoping the smoke wouldn't reach that far.

Firefighter Richard Harden helped put out the fire. Then he helped remove the bodies. The tale of *terror* still showed on the victims' faces. "Some looked *horrified*," he said. "Some looked like they were in shock. There were some people holding hands. Some people had torn their clothes off in their panic to get out."

The Happy Land fire was the worst fire New York City had seen in a long time. [The worst ever had occurred exactly 79 years earlier. On March 25, 1911, the Triangle Shirtwaist factory had caught fire. That blaze killed 146 women. They, too, were mostly immigrants.]

Five people made it out of Happy Land alive. These five found a seldom-used door on the first floor. Outside, a gate blocked their

---

消防队员理查德·哈登先是参与灭火，然后又协助清运尸体。恐怖的情景仍然可以从受害者的面部表情上反映出来。他说："有些人好像很慌张，还有人好像很惊讶，很多人高举双手。在惊慌逃走的过程中，有人衣服都被刮破了。"

欢乐谷的火灾是纽约很长时间以来最严重的一次。（历史上，最严重的一起火灾发生在整整79年前。1911年3月25日，三角衬衫厂发生火灾，共造成146名妇女死亡。他们中多数也是移民。）

有5人在欢乐谷火灾中死里逃生。这5个人在一楼发现一扇平时很少开启的门，外面还有一扇大门拦路。他们想方设法打开大门，逃了出来。

---

terror n. 恐怖　　　　　　　　　　horrified adj. 惊恐的；惊骇的

escape. They managed to force it open and get away. One of the five was Julio Gonzalez's ex-girlfriend, Lydia Feliciano.

Meanwhile, back in his room, Gonzalez went to bed. The police *arrested* him there later in the day. Gonzalez quickly admitted his *guilt*. When he realized what he had done, he began to cry. "I got angry," he said. "The devil got into me." His tears may have been sincere. But they couldn't bring back the 87 people who died in the Happy Land Club.

---

其中之一就是朱力奥·冈萨雷斯的前女友丽达·菲利西诺。

这个时候，冈萨雷斯已经回到自己家中睡觉去了。就在当天，警察将他逮捕。冈萨雷斯很快认罪伏法。当意识到自己所做的一切之后，他痛哭起来。他说："我非常恼怒，然后就失去了理智。"他的泪水可能是真诚的，但是那些泪水无法挽回欢乐谷夜总会里的87条生命。

---

arrest *v.* 逮捕　　　　　　　　　　　　　　guilt *n.* 犯罪；过失

TOTAL PANIC

# 5

# A Deadly Plunge

A thick fog had moved in. Willie Odom could barely see through the *gloomy* darkness. Odom was at the wheel of the tugboat Mauvilla. He was pushing a string of six *barges* up the Mobile River. At least, he thought he was on the Mobile River. Odom did not realize it, but he had taken a wrong turn.

*Rescue teams drag the remains of the Sunset Limited out of the Big Bayou Canot in Alabama. The train had been carrying 210 sleeping passengers through a foggy night when disaster suddenly struck.*

## 致命陷阱

救援人员把"急速落日"号列车的残骸从阿拉巴马州大拜优克努特河中打捞上来。在雾色朦胧的深夜里行进的列车上睡着210名乘客。这时，灾难突然从天而降。

浓雾笼罩在阴沉的夜色中，威利·奥德姆几乎什么都看不见。他正驾驶着"莫维拉"号拖轮。船上拴着一条绳子，他正要把六艘泊船拖到莫拜尔河。至少，他以为他在莫拜尔河上。奥德姆没有意识到他走错了方向。现在"莫维拉"号已经驶入大拜优克努特河中。在阿拉巴马州的这条小河

---

gloomy  adj.  阴沉的；黑暗的                                    barge  n.  驳船

◆ A DEADLY PLUNGE

The Mauvilla was now in Big Bayou Canot. Tugs weren't supposed to be in this small Alabama river. The barges they pushed were too large for Big Bayou.

As Odom moved upstream, he felt a sudden *bump*. "It wasn't [a] real hard bump," he later said. "[But] it wasn't a real soft bump." Odom figured one of the barges might have hit some small log or piece of *debris*. But it was worse than that—much worse. One of the barges had hit a low-hanging railroad bridge. The bridge was knocked 70 feet out of *alignment*. That meant the train tracks now ran straight into the *murky* river. In just a couple of minutes, a train would come speeding down these very tracks.

It was September 22, 1993. At 2:53 A.M., a train did approach the bridge. It was an Amtrak train called the Sunset Limited. It was

---

里，拖轮是行驶不开的。对于大拜优克努特河而言，拖轮牵引着的这些泊船实在太庞大了。

正当奥德姆驶船逆流而上时，他忽然觉得撞到了什么东西。他后来说道"这次撞击算不上剧烈，但也绝不是很轻微的。" 奥德姆以为有一艘驳船撞到了河里漂着的小块木头或其他什么破碎了的东西。但情况比他想象的还要糟糕——而且糟糕得多。有一艘泊船撞到了距离河面很近的一座铁路桥上。桥梁被撞离直线，跑出70英尺开外，由此导致上面的铁轨直直地伸进了浑黑的河水中。几分钟后，有一列火车将会顺着这些铁轨冲进河中。

1993年9月22日，深夜2点53分，一列火车开到桥边。这列火车属于全美铁路客运公司，名为"急速落日"号，此时上面有210名乘客，正以

---

bump  *n.* 碰撞  
alignment  *n.* 成直线

debris  *n.* 碎片；残骸  
murky  *adj.* 黑暗的；浑浊的

## TOTAL PANIC

carrying 210 people. The train was zipping along at 70 miles per hour. Without warning, it hit the broken tracks. Three engines and four of the train's cars plunged off the bridge and burst into flames. The four remaining cars derailed and jammed into each other on the tracks above. One car was left hanging, half in the water, half in the air.

The crash sent everyone *sprawling*. Conductor Gary Lee Farmer was at the back of the train. He was with crew member Dwight Thompson. Farmer later talked about the crash. "It was like flying into the side of a mountain," he said. "There was a *horrendous* impact. I was sliding down the aisle on my stomach. Mr. Thompson came sailing over my head."

Farmer grabbed his radio. He sent out a distress call. Then he began working his way to the front of the train. He wanted to check

---

每小时70英里的速度前进着。列车没有收到任何警报，直接冲向已被损坏的铁轨。3节机车和4节车厢掉入河中，发生爆炸并起火燃烧。其余4节车厢冲出铁轨，因相互碰撞而最终堆叠在一起。有一节车厢悬在那里，一半在水中，一半在空中。

事故的发生使得车厢里一片狼藉。列车长加里·李·法莫此时正在列车尾部。他正和列车员德怀特·汤普森在一起。后来，法莫谈起了这次坠车事故。他说道："我们好像碰到山上，真是一次可怕的撞击。我头朝下摔倒了，幸好汤普森先生过来扶住了我的脑袋。"

法莫抓起无线电发报机，发出了遇险求救信号。然后他跑到列车前

---

sprawling *adj.* 杂乱无序伸展的     horrendous *adj.* 可怕的

◆ A DEADLY PLUNGE

out the damage. He wanted to see if there was anything he could do to help.

In the cars still on the bridge, Farmer said, "It was sheer *chaos*. People were all over the place." As he neared the front cars, he saw that a diesel-fuel fire had broken out on the surface of the water. It threatened to spread to the rest of the train. Meanwhile, the car that was *dangling* in the air was beginning to sink down. Some people were in the water. They were screaming, splashing. One elderly woman was being carried downstream.

With no thought for his own safety, Farmer jumped into the oily water. He rescued the woman. Then he tried to save those still trapped in the sinking car. But he couldn't get the car door open. The thought of people dying on the other side of that door upset him

---

面，想查看受损情况。他想看看是否能够实施一些应急措施。

法莫说："在铁路桥上的车厢里，一片混乱，人们东倒西歪。"由于法莫就站在车厢前门旁边，他看到了河面上因柴油泄露所引燃的大火，火势有蔓延到列车其他部分的危险。与此同时，悬在半空中的车厢也开始下沉。有些人已经浸在了水中，他们高声呼叫，并且拍打水面，有一位老妇人已经被冲到下游去了。

法莫不顾个人安危，跳进充满油污的河水中，他把那位妇人救了上来，然后开始营救那些仍被困在下沉车厢中的人们。但是他打不开车厢

---

chaos  n.  混乱                                                      dangle  v.  悬荡

## TOTAL PANIC

badly. "That will *haunt* me for the rest of my life," he said.

Farmer was one hero. There were others. Those who were not badly hurt did their best to help. Charlie Jones, a waiter on the train, had been sleeping. The crash caused the *bunk* above him to break off the wall. It fell on top of Jones. "Somehow, I was able to get out from under [the bunk]," he said.

But then he heard a voice calling out from the next *compartment*. "I can't get out! My door won't open! I can't get out! Please help me, I'm beginning to burn." It was one of Jones's friends. Jones struggled to get the door open, but it was just not possible. The door wouldn't *budge*; it was jammed shut. "I tried hard to get him out," said Jones later. "It was no use." Finally, the smoke became too intense. Despite his brave effort, Jones had to leave his friend

---

门。眼看着车门另一边垂死挣扎着的人们却又无能为力，这种感觉对他来说实在太糟糕了。他说："我这辈子都忘不了那种感觉。"

法莫是个英雄，其他人也同样是英雄。那些伤势不算太重的人也拼尽全力营救其他人。列车上的一名服务员查理·琼斯正在睡梦之中。列车的突然坠落使上面的铺位从墙上脱落，砸到他身上。他说："不知道是怎么弄的，我竟然能从那里爬出来。"

但随即他就听到隔壁传来的呼救声。"我出不去了！门打不开！我出不去了！帮帮我，我要被烧死了！"呼救的人是琼斯的一个朋友。琼斯拼尽全力要把那扇门打开，但这是根本不可能的。门纹丝不动，已经被堵死了。琼斯后来说："我想把他救出来，费了很大力气，但毫无作用。"后来，烟尘

---

haunt *v.* 缠绕；萦绕
compartment *n.* 隔间

bunk *n.* 铺位；床铺
budge *v.* 移动

◆ A DEADLY PLUNGE

behind.

Michael Dopheide had more success. The 26-year-old Dopheide was in the car that ended up half in the water. He had been asleep when the train ran off the bridge. The impact *hurled* him to the floor. Dopheide *stumbled* to his feet. It was dark. Earlier, he had stashed his glasses in his boots, and he didn't have time to look for them. A wooden piling had broken one of the windows. Muddy water was rushing into the car. Already the water was up to his waist. Dopheide knew he had to act quickly. He heard a woman shouting, "Oh God, we're all gonna die!"

Somehow Dopheide found the emergency exit. With help from some other people, he removed the window from the exit door. Then he jumped into the water. He turned his attention to saving others.

---

实在是太强烈了。尽管琼斯很勇敢，但最终他没能救出他的朋友。

迈克尔·杜费尔德遇到的情况就比琼斯幸运得多。当时，26岁的杜费尔德就在那节一半已经掉进河里的车厢之中。列车坠桥时他正在睡觉。冲击作用让他滚落下来，摔倒在地面上。一片漆黑，眼镜掉到靴子里，他也没时间去找了。有一扇窗户被木桩打碎了，泥水涌进车厢。积水已经齐腰深了，杜费尔德知道必须赶快离开这里。这时他听到一位妇人的叫喊："天哪！我们要死了！"

杜费尔德不知怎么找到了紧急出口。在其他人的帮助下，他把那扇窗户从安全出口移开，然后跳进水中。杜费尔德开始帮助营救其他人。不能

---

hurl  *v.*  猛投；猛摔                    stumble  *v.*  绊倒

## TOTAL PANIC

There was no time to waste. Anyone left in the car would soon drown.

From the exit door, it was a six-foot drop to the water. Some people were afraid to jump that far. Some were afraid of the snakes and *alligators* that were known to live in the bayou. And some did not want to jump because they could not swim. Yet, one after another, Dopheide *coaxed* people into the water. Donnie Hughes was one of those people. She couldn't swim. As she perched in the metal frame of the exit door, she froze. "Then I looked below and saw [Dopheide]. He was saying, 'It's OK. I'm here, come on, I've got ya.'" Hughes did jump, and Dopheide pulled her to safety. In all, he saved more than 30 lives.

---

再浪费时间了，一旦留在车厢内，人们马上就会被里面的水吞没。

太平门距离水面有6英尺远。有人不敢跳这么高，有人害怕河里的蛇和美洲鳄，还有人不想跳，因为他们不会游泳。但不管怎么说，在杜费尔德的劝导下，人们还是一个挨一个跳进水中。唐尼·休斯就是人群中的一员。她不会游泳，站在门框那儿呆住了。"然后我往下面看，看到了杜费尔德，他说'没事儿！我在这儿！过来，我接着你！'"休斯跳了下去，杜费尔德抓住了她，一切平安无事。杜费尔德总共救出了三十多人。

---

alligator *n.* 短吻鳄　　　　　　　　　　　　　　　　coax *v.* 劝诱

◆ A DEADLY PLUNGE

Back on the Mauvilla, Willie Odom realized what had happened. He turned his *tug* around and came to help. But the heat and flames kept him from getting too close. Still, Odom lowered two small boats and some life jackets into the water. Dopheide lifted several people up to him. One was a two-year-old girl. Another was an elderly lady. A third was a *crippled* child. Odom knew his wrong turn had caused this. All he could say to these people was, "I'm sorry."

It took hours to rescue all the survivors. The bridge was in a remote area. The nearest road was six miles away. Helicopters had to wait until dawn for the fog to clear. At long last, help did arrive. But it was too late for 47 people. The fog, the fire—and human error— had combined to create the worst accident in the history of Amtrak.

---

再说"莫维拉"号拖轮，威利·奥德姆意识到发生了什么事情。他调转了航向，然后参与到营救中，但是他被高温和烈火所阻，难以靠近。尽管如此，他还是把两条小船和一些救生衣放入河中。杜费尔德把几个人举到奥德姆面前，其中有一个两岁大的小姑娘，一位老妇人，还有一个跛脚的小孩子。奥德姆知道是他的误判航向导致了这一切的发生。对这些受害者，他只能说："真对不起！"

营救工作花费了好几个小时。这座桥地处偏远，最近的公路也在6英里开外。直到破晓时分，浓雾散尽，直升飞机才飞了过来，很久以后，救援队伍才抵达现场。但是对于47名遇难者而言，这一切来得都太迟了。浓雾、大火、人为失误，所有这些因素叠加起来，造成了全美铁路客运公司有史以来最为严重的一起事故。

---

tug *n.* 拖船　　　　　　　　　　　　　　　　　　　cripple *v.* 使跛

## TOTAL PANIC

# 6

# Nightmare in the Twin Towers

It had been a great field trip. The 17 six-year-olds had just seen all of New York City. They had viewed it from the top of the World Trade Center. The center has two huge *towers*. Each rises 110 *stories* into the air. The children had been at the top of the south tower.

Now they were headed back down.

*The World Trade Center in New York City was rocked by a terrorist bomb blast on February 26, 1993. Emergency workers rushed to the scene to rescue the approximately 100,000 people inside.*

---

## 世贸噩梦

1993年2月26日，纽约世界贸易中心遭到恐怖炸弹袭击。救援人员冲入事发现场，总共救出约十万人。

这真是一次难忘的实地考察。17个6岁大的孩子刚刚看遍纽约全城。他们站在世界贸易中心楼顶，俯瞰这座城市。世界贸易中心由两栋摩天大厦组成，每一栋都有110层高，伸入云端。此时，孩子们正在南面的那座大厦上。

现在孩子们正在下楼。他们甚至在坐电梯时都是那么的兴奋。电梯预计运行时间仅为90秒。事后证明，这次运行时间长了很多。并且，这次乘

---

tower *n.* 高楼　　　　　　　　　　　story(US)=storey *n.* 楼层

◆ NIGHTMARE IN THE TWIN TOWERS

For them, even an elevator ride was thrilling. The ride was supposed to take just 90 seconds. As it turned out, though, it took much longer. And it was more than a thrill. It was a nightmare.

The date was February 26, 1993. The teacher led the children into the elevator. It was a big car, 10 feet by 20 feet. But there were lots of other people going down. By the time the doors closed, the car was very full. There were 72 people inside. "We were really *squashed*," said one woman, who was helping with the field trip. "But we only thought it was going to be a few minutes."

The kids began counting the floors as they zipped past. Halfway down, the lights over the door *flickered* and died. "Then all of a sudden—boom!" said one passenger. It was exactly 12:18 P.M.. "[The elevator] stopped. All the kids screamed." The car was stuck between the 36th and the 35th floors.

---

坐电梯的经历并不令人兴奋，那简直就是一场噩梦。

时间是1993年2月26日。老师把孩子们领进电梯。电梯内部空间很大，足有10英尺宽，20英尺长。但是其他很多人也上了电梯。电梯门关闭的时候，轿厢已经十分拥挤了，里面共有72人。一位协助这次实地考察的妇人说道："人都快被挤坏了，但我们以为这只是几分钟的事情。"

孩子们开始数着下落的楼层。下到半途中时，轿厢门上的灯光闪动了一下后就熄灭了。电梯里一位乘客说："然后，突然之间——轰隆隆！电梯停住了。孩子们都惊叫起来。"时间是中午12时18分，轿厢卡在了36楼和35楼之间。

---

squash *v.* 挤压           flicker *v.* 闪烁

**TOTAL PANIC**

There was no room to move about. The car was pitch black. The only light came from cigarette lighters. The adults tried to calm the small children. A few older children in the car, however, started to panic. One cried, "I am going to die. That's it. I am going to die."

To distract the kids, the adults led them in song. The children sang everything they knew. They sang alphabet songs. They sang holiday songs. They also sang the theme song from the TV show Barney. The kids did their best to belt out, "I love you, you love me, we're a happy family."

With so many people packed together, the car grew hotter and hotter. Then, somehow, the passengers pried the doors open a bit. That let in some fresh air. But it also *revealed* a terrible sight. Smoke was curling up the elevator *shaft*. Now, even some of the adults began to lose hope. "I thought we were all going to die," said one

---

根本没有走动的地方。轿厢里漆黑一团，仅有的一点光芒来自点烟用的打火机。大人们想让小孩子保持镇静。但是，轿厢里几个大一点的孩子却开始发慌，几个孩子嚷道："我快死了！是的，我快死了！"

为了转移孩子们的注意力，大人们领着他们唱起歌来。孩子们把所会的歌唱了个遍：他们唱字母歌，唱节日歌，唱巴尼电视秀的主题歌。孩子们扯着嗓子唱道："我爱你们，你们也爱我，我们共有欢乐的大家庭。"

这么多人挤在一起，轿厢里变得越来越热。后来人们想方设法把轿厢门扒开了一丝缝隙，这样可以吹进来一点新鲜空气。但是，透过缝隙，外面可怕的场景也展示在人们面前：浓烟顺着电梯的垂直升降井涌了上来。现在，甚至一部分成年人都开始绝望了。一位乘客说："我认为大家都快要死了。"

---

reveal  v. 展现；显露出                    shaft  n. （电梯的）升降机井

◆ NIGHTMARE IN THE TWIN TOWERS

passenger.

At last, after four long hours, rescue workers reached the car. They passed a flashlight inside. Then they set up a special ladder to get people out. It was a slow and difficult job. One hour later, just 10 children had been *retrieved*. Luckily, at that point, the car came to life again. It slowly resumed its downward journey. When it reached the ground floor, everyone inside shouted for joy. Few people have ever been happier to get out of an elevator.

But shocking news *awaited* them. The car had not stopped because of a power outage. It had not stopped because of some faulty part. It was far worse than that. There had been a huge explosion at the base of the tower. Terrorists had tried to blow up the World Trade Center.

They had almost succeeded. Two men had driven a rented van

---

最后，经历了漫长的4个小时之后，救援队伍来到轿厢前。他们递进去一个手电筒，然后竖起了一架特制的梯子，以便里面的人能够爬出来。这是一项进展缓慢而又十分困难的工作。一个小时过去了，仅有10个孩子被救出来。所幸的是，此时轿厢终于恢复正常，重新开始缓慢地向下运行。轿厢到达一楼时，人们欢呼起来，能从电梯里出来了，很多人都从来没有这么高兴过。

但是令人震惊的消息传了过来。是由于电力的不足和某些部件的损坏，轿厢不能够停下来。事实上，情况比这还要糟糕。双子大厦的最底部发生了剧烈爆炸。恐怖分子企图引爆整个世界贸易中心。

恐怖分子几乎就要得逞了。有两个人驾驶着一辆租来的货车冲进地下

---

retrieve *v.* 挽救；恢复　　　　　　　　　　　　　　await *v.* 等待

**TOTAL PANIC**

into the underground garage. They had with them a 1,200-pound bomb. They planted the bomb in the garage, then took off. The bomb exploded at 12:18.

The World Trade Center is like a small city. Every day 130,000 people go there to work or visit. The bombers had hoped to bring down the whole complex. That was why they used such a huge bomb. The blast was enormous. It *swayed* all 110 stories of both towers. It left a crater 200 feet by 100 feet. The hole was five stories deep. Yet mercifully, neither tower *collapsed*.

Six people died in the blast. Given the bomb's size, it was a miracle that more didn't die. One firefighter stared in wonder at the massive crater. It was a sight he wouldn't soon forget. "It looked like a giant barbecue pit with coals burning," he said.

The blast injured more than 1,000 people. It blew out windows.

---

车库，随身携带着一枚重达1200磅的炸弹。他们打算在车库内引爆炸弹后逃走。爆炸时间正是12时18分。

世界贸易中心就像是一座小型城市。每天有13万人到那里工作或者前去参观。实施爆炸的人想把这里搅得天翻地覆，这就是他们使用如此巨型的炸弹的原因。爆炸非常剧烈，撼动了两座摩天大厦的全部110层楼，并且炸出一个200英尺长，100英尺宽的弹坑，深度相当于5层楼高。所幸两座大厦都没有倒塌。

爆炸造成6人丧生。那么巨大的一枚炸弹却没有造成更多人员死亡，这真是一个奇迹。一名消防队员盯着现场的巨大弹坑发愣。他永远也忘不了那一幕。他说："就像一次盛大的午餐之后，现场着火了，烧出了一个大坑。"

爆炸造成一千多人受伤。爆炸震碎了玻璃，并使得灯光熄灭，电力中

---

sway *v.* 动摇        collapse *v.* 倒塌

◆ NIGHTMARE IN THE TWIN TOWERS

It knocked out the lights and power in both towers. All the backup systems were *ruined* too. The blast shook marble *slabs* loose. Steam pipes *ruptured*, spewing hot mist into the air. Fires broke out. And thick, black smoke was drawn up through the stairways until it reached the top floors. One worker was on the 105th floor at the time of the blast. "All the computers shut down. All the phones shut down," he said. "Then all of a sudden we saw smoke everywhere."

Some people broke windows to let in fresh air. That was not a good idea. It vented the smoke, making it spread faster. Also, the pieces of broken glass injured people on the streets below.

It was even worse in the basement of the twin towers. Joseph Cacciatore worked there. The blast was so strong that it knocked out his contact lenses. It also shattered his eye socket. His face was *splattered* with blood. In the darkness, Cacciatore wasn't sure how

---

断。全部备用设施化为乌有，连大理石板都被震碎了。水汽管道破裂，热气喷涌而出。浓厚的黑烟顺着楼道一直涌到顶层。爆炸时，一名工人就在第一百〇五层楼上。他说："所有电脑都停机了，所有的电话都断线了。然后，我突然发现到处都是黑烟。"

有人砸碎窗户，让新鲜空气透进来。这并不是一个好主意，因为它使烟气得以流通，而扩散得更为迅速。并且，掉落的玻璃碎片也砸伤了楼下街道上的行人。

双子大厦底部的情况更加糟糕。朱瑟夫·凯奇特里就在那里工作。爆炸太强烈了，震碎了他的隐形眼镜，也伤到了他的眼睛。他满脸是血。在

---

ruin *v.* 毁灭
rupture *v.* 破裂

slab *n.* 厚板
splatter *v.* 溅泼

## TOTAL PANIC

badly he had been hurt. But he knew he wasn't the only one injured. All around him he could hear people screaming.

Firefighter Kevin Shea went to check out the parking garage. But the bomb had weakened the floor. As he inched his way along, the *concrete* gave way. Shea fell four floors. Incredibly, he wasn't killed. He landed on a pile of heavy cardboard, breaking only his left knee and right foot. Still, he thought he would die. "Rocks and *cinders* were falling everywhere," he said later. "I thought, 'This is it.' I prayed to God to take me quick."

The bomb rocked more than the World Trade Center. It rocked the nation. Americans were horrified by the attack. They pressed police to find out who had done this evil deed.

The police soon had the answer. A group of Muslim militants was arrested. Their leader was Sheik Omar Abdel-Rahman. He was a

---

黑暗中，他不能确定自己的伤势有多重，但是他知道自己并不是唯一受伤的人。他听到周围的人都在哭喊。

消防队员凯文·西去车库查看那里的情况。但是爆炸使得地板非常脆弱。他顺着混凝土地面慢慢向前挪动，然后就失足跌下了四层楼。令人难以置信的是，他没有死。他掉到一个厚纸板堆上，只摔坏了左膝和右脚。即使这样，他也以为自己将不久于人世。后来，他说道："碎石和灰渣掉得到处都是，我心想'完蛋了'，然后就祈求上帝快点把我召过去。"

这次爆炸震惊了世界贸易中心，也震惊了全国。美国人被这次袭击吓坏了。他们向警方施压，要求追查出元凶。

警方很快给出了答案，一批穆斯林好战分子被捕。他们的头目是奥马

---

concrete  n.  混凝土            cinder  n.  煤渣；炭渣

### ◆ NIGHTMARE IN THE TWIN TOWERS

*preacher* who had always hated the United States. He had urged his followers to wage "holy war." The World Trade Center was just for starters. He had plans to blow up other New York City landmarks, as well. One was the United Nations building. Others were the Lincoln and Holland tunnels and the George Washington Bridge.

In the fall of 1993, 10 Muslims were brought to *trial*. The court found all of them guilty. Abdel-Rahman got life in prison. The nine other plotters received 25 years to life in prison. But the damage was done. The World Trade Center had to be closed for a month. And the memory of the bombing lingered long beyond that.

---

尔·亚伯德-拉曼酋长，一位始终憎恨着美国的伊斯兰教徒。他号召追随者们发动"圣战"。世界贸易中心的惨案仅仅是开端，他已经计划针对纽约城的其他标志性建筑物实施爆炸，其中之一是联合国大厦，还有林肯-荷兰登隧道，以及乔治·华盛顿大桥。

1993年的秋天，10名穆斯林恐怖分子被送上法庭，接受审判。法庭宣判他们全部有罪。亚伯德-拉曼只能在监狱中度过余生，其他9名同案犯被判处25年以上直至终身监禁。但是世界贸易中心的破坏已经成为事实，那里不得不关门一个月。而爆炸给人们留下的记忆将持续更长的时间。

---

preacher *n.* 传教士；牧师    trial *n.* 审讯；审判

## TOTAL PANIC

# 7

# Stay Out of the Water!

We will never know what Charles Vansant was thinking as he *splashed* in the water on that hot summer day. But chances are, he wasn't thinking about sharks. Most people in 1916 knew little about sharks. Many people believed that sharks were as *harmless* as other fish in

*In the summer of 1916, some swimmers in New Jersey had a rare—and unwelcome—encounter with the most feared of all ocean fish: sharks. It is believed that the attackers included both bull sharks and great white sharks.*

---

## 严禁下水

1916年夏季，一些正在新泽西海滨游泳的人罕见地——也是极不情愿地——遭遇到最可怕的海洋鱼类——鲨鱼。人们确信实施这次攻击的包括公牛鲨和大白鲨。

我们永远不可能知道在那个炎热的夏天，在水中挣扎的查尔斯·文森特头脑里正在想些什么。但是，当时他很可能根本没想到水里会有鲨鱼。1916年时，人们对鲨鱼还知之甚少。很多人以为鲨鱼和海洋里其他鱼类

---

splash v. 溅；泼；激起浪花　　　　　　　　harmless adj. 无害的

◆ STAY OUT OF THE WATER!

the sea. Besides, people thought, sharks stayed in warm water. One would never travel as far north as, say, New Jersey.

Vansant took his swim at 5:00 P.M. on July 2, 1916. He was at Beach Haven, New Jersey. A man named Sheridan Taylor saw him standing alone in five feet of water. All at once, Vansant screamed. He began to beat the water wildly. Taylor saw the water around Vansant turn red. Quickly, Taylor swam out to help. As he drew near, he saw a *shark* biting into Vansant's leg. Taylor and some other men managed to drag Vansant to the beach. But it was too late. Charles Vansant died within a few hours.

Taylor and the other rescuers saw the shark clearly. They described it as 10 feet long and *bluish*-gray. But experts dismissed the men's claim. These experts said it could not possibly have been

---

一样，是不会伤害人类的。此外，人们认为鲨鱼只生活在温暖的水域中，不会游到非常偏北，比如新泽西这样的地方。

　　1916年7月2日，下午5:00，在新泽西州黑文海滩，文森特开始游泳。有个名叫谢里丹·泰勒的男子看见他独自停留在5英尺深的水中。突然，文森特发出惊叫声，并开始疯狂地拍打水面。泰勒看到文森特周围的海水都变红了，立即游过去救他。来到近处，泰勒发现一条鲨鱼咬住了文森特的腿。泰勒，还有另外几个人，设法把文森特拖到了海滩上，但为时已晚。几个小时之后，查尔斯·文森特还是死了。

　　泰勒和另外几个去营救文森特的人清楚地看到了那条鲨鱼。据他们描述，那条鲨鱼有10英尺长，身上是蓝灰色的。但是专家们不相信这是真

---

shark  n.  鲨鱼　　　　　　　　　　　　bluish  adj.  带蓝色的

**TOTAL PANIC**

a shark. Surely, they said, the men were mistaken. Surely it had been some other kind of fish.

Four days later, a man named Charles Bruder went swimming at a beach called Spring Lake. It was 35 miles north of Beach Haven. Without warning, Bruder, too, was struck by a shark. It attacked his right leg, biting the *limb* off just below the knee. The shark then ripped into Bruder's left leg. Rescuers got him to shore. But, again, it was too late. Bruder bled to death on the beach.

In the days following Bruder's death, the people of New Jersey grew *frantic*. Two people were dead, and the killer or killers were still at large. Most residents refused to return to the water. Officials tried to calm everyone's nerves. They put up wire nets along the beaches to keep sharks out. People began to patrol the shore in boats. They

---

的，专家们认为这里不可能有鲨鱼出没，一定是那几个人弄错了，他们看到的肯定是另外的某种鱼类。

4天之后，一位名叫查尔斯·布鲁德的男子在春湖海滩游泳。这里地处黑文海滩以北35英里。同样是在毫无警觉的情况下，布鲁德被一条鲨鱼攻击了。鲨鱼先是攻击他的右腿，把膝盖以下的部分全部咬了下来，然后又咬裂了他的左腿。营救人员把他拖到岸上，但还是迟了一步。在海滩上，布鲁德失血过多，最终死亡。

在布鲁德死后的一段时间里，新泽西人惶惶不可终日。死了两个人，可是杀人元凶仍然逍遥法外。大多数居民都不敢再下水了。政府官员们力图平息人们的紧张情绪。他们沿着海岸竖起铁丝网，把鲨鱼挡在外面。人

---

limb  *n.*  肢；臂                    frantic  *adj.*  狂暴的；狂乱的

◆ STAY OUT OF THE WATER!

carried rifles, spears, and *dynamite*. Even so, most people didn't feel safe. Most swimmers stayed out of the ocean.

Meanwhile, the experts continued to get it wrong. Some still doubted that the killer was a shark. They said it might have been a very large *turtle* or a huge *mackerel*. Frank Claret, a boat captain, said he had never seen a man-eating shark north of the Bahamas. Olympic swimmer Annette Kellerman also spoke out on the subject. She proclaimed, "The shark, no matter what species he belongs to, is at heart an arrant *coward*..."

Still, most people scanned the shore nervously. Some headed inland. They cooled off in rivers and bays. On July 12, Thomas Cottrell was fishing in Matawan Creek. He noticed a "dark, gray shape" moving through the water at a fast rate. Cottrell rushed

---

们开始坐着小艇沿着海岸巡逻。他们端着步枪、拿着长矛、装好炸药。即使这样，多数人还是觉得不安全。大多数游泳者也远离了海洋。

与此同时，专家们仍坚持着他们的错误判断。有些专家仍对元凶是鲨鱼表示怀疑，他们认为那可能是一只大海龟或者一条巨大的鲭鱼。船长弗兰克·克莱瑞特表示，他从未在巴哈马群岛以北见过食人鲨。奥运会游泳选手安妮特·凯勒曼也说出了自己的看法。她宣称："鲨鱼，不论具体属于哪一种，其实都是彻头彻尾的胆小鬼……"

尽管如此，大多数人还是在海滨紧张地巡视。有些人转移到内陆活动，在河流里，港湾中，人们才算平静下来。7月12日那天，托马斯·科特雷尔正在马塔万河边钓鱼。他注意到一个"阴暗的，灰色的东西"快速

---

dynamite *n.* 炸药
mackerel *n.* 鲭鱼
turtle *n.* 海龟
coward *n.* 懦夫；胆怯者

**TOTAL PANIC**

into town to warn people that a shark was in the creek. But the townspeople merely laughed at him. The *creek* was 10 miles from the open ocean. How could any shark get that far inland? Besides, it was a hot day. Many people were determined to cool down in Matawan Creek.

Twelve-year-old Lester Stilwell was one of those people. Stilwell and some other boys took off for a swim in the creek. They decided to swim off an old pier. Stilwell was a strong swimmer. So he swam out further than his friends. Suddenly, out of nowhere, a shark grabbed the boy and pulled him down. When Stilwell surfaced again, he was flailing his arms and screaming. His body was *swirling* around and around in the water.

Stanley Fisher, aged 24, was standing nearby. He saw Stilwell

---

地从水中穿过。科特雷尔冲进城里，警告人们那条河里有鲨鱼。但市民们仅仅是把他嘲笑了一番。这条河远离海洋足有10英里。鲨鱼怎么可能游到内陆这么远的地方来呢？另外，天气炎热，很多人都决定去马塔万河消暑。

　　12岁的莱斯特·斯蒂维尔就是这些人中的一员。斯蒂维尔和其他一些男孩子跑到马塔万河游泳。他们打算游到一个旧码头去。斯蒂维尔水性非常好，所以比他的伙伴们游得更远。突然间，不知从何处冒出来一只鲨鱼，拽住他，并且把他拖到水下。当斯蒂维尔再次浮出水面时，他用力挥动胳膊并且大声呼救。他的身子在河水中来回转圈。

　　24岁的斯坦利·费舍尔当时就在附近。他看到斯蒂维尔正在水中挣

---

creek  *n.*  小河；小溪　　　　　　　　　　　　　　　　　swirl  *v.*  旋转

◆ STAY OUT OF THE WATER!

struggling. Quickly Fisher ran to the edge of the creek. As he *dashed* past a woman, she shouted, "Remember what Cottrell said! It may have been a shark!"

"A shark here?" answered Fisher in disbelief. "I don't care, anyway. I'm going after that boy!"

Fisher jumped into his bathing suit and swam out to Stilwell. By then, the boy had been dragged underwater again. Fisher dove down, searching for him. At last he came up to the surface, shouting, "I've got him!" By that time, Fisher was close to the opposite shore, so that's where he headed with the lifeless body of Lester Stilwell. He almost made it. His feet touched the bottom of the creek. Then, in one terrible flash, the shark attacked him. People watching on the opposite shore saw Fisher throw up his arms and *yell*. With its teeth

---

扎，马上跑到河边。当他冲过一位妇人身边时，这位妇人喊道："记住科特雷尔说的话！那可能是一条鲨鱼！"

"河里有鲨鱼？"费舍尔不太相信，"但是管不了那么多了，我得赶快去救孩子！"

费舍尔穿上游泳衣，跳进河里，向斯蒂维尔游了过去。此时，孩子已经又一次被拖进水里。费舍尔俯冲下去找他。最后，费舍尔游出水面高喊："我找到他了！"当时，费舍尔距离河对岸很近，于是他拖着奄奄一息的莱斯特·斯蒂维尔向对岸游去。他快要游到地方了，脚已经踩到河底。突然，就在这一瞬间可怕的事情发生了，鲨鱼向他发起了攻击。正在河对岸观望的人们看到费舍尔高举双臂，大声呼救。鲨鱼用利齿咬住费舍

---

dash *v.* 猛冲　　　　　　　　　　　　　　　　　　yell *v.* 叫喊

**TOTAL PANIC**

locked into his flesh, the shark dragged Fisher underwater.

Other men, who were rushing to help in motorboats, managed to pull Fisher out of the water. He was still alive, but he was in shock. His right leg had been torn to *shreds*. There was no flesh left between his waist and knee. Fisher *mumbled* a few words, saying he had thought he was safe when his feet touched bottom. He died before reaching the hospital.

People were in a *frenzy*. Word of the shark attacks traveled like lightning up and down the banks of the creek. Everyone scrambled to get out of the water. John Dunn, aged 12, and some friends were diving off a pier when they heard the news. They hurried to climb to safety. Dunn was the last one out. With just his left leg still in the water, he felt a shark grab him. The *creature* tore away most of the

---

尔，把他拖进水中。

  一位男子开着摩托艇前去救援。他想方设法把费舍尔拉出了水面。费舍尔还活着，但精神受到了巨大的刺激。他的右腿血肉模糊，腰部和膝盖之间的肉已经被咬光了。费舍尔艰难地低语了几句，说他在脚踩到河底的时候就以为自己已经安全了。在被送往医院的途中，费舍尔不治身亡。

  人们都要发疯了。鲨鱼来袭的消息闪电般地传遍了这条河两岸。人们争相逃出水面。12岁的约翰·达恩和几个朋友听到这个消息的时候正在游向码头的途中。为了安全起见，他们匆忙爬上岸来。达恩是最后一个爬上来的。当左腿还在河里的时候，他感到自己被一只鲨鱼咬住了。这个家伙

---

shred   *n.*   碎片         mumble   *v.*   含糊地说
frenzy   *n.*   疯狂        creature   *n.*   生物

◆ STAY OUT OF THE WATER!

boy's leg. Dunn was taken to the hospital. He lived, but his leg had to be *amputated*.

The attacks in Matawan Creek set off a massive shark hunt. Hundreds of hunters took to the water in boats. They armed themselves with nets, dynamite, guns, and hooks. Over the next two days, they *scoured* the New Jersey coastline. They managed to kill several sharks. One was an eight-and-one-half-foot great white shark. In its stomach lay human bones and *flesh*. One bone was *identified* as the shinbone of Charles Bruder.

So there was no doubt about it: a shark really was to blame for the recent deaths. But was there only one killer, or were there others? At the time, most people thought all the attacks were the work of one crazed shark. We now know that that is not likely. A great

---

几乎把孩子的左腿咬了下去。达恩被送往医院。他幸存下来，但是他的左腿必须截掉了。

　　马塔万河的袭击事件引发了一次针对鲨鱼的大搜捕行动。几百名捕猎者坐船下水，带着渔网、炸药、枪支和钓钩。两天之内，他们急速搜遍了新泽西的海岸，并想方设法捕杀掉了几条鲨鱼，其中有一条八英尺半长的大白鲨。人们在这条大白鲨的胃里发现了人的骨骼和肌肉。经过辨认，其中就有一块是查尔斯·布鲁德的胫骨。

　　因此，毫无疑问，制造最近发生的致人死亡事件的凶手确实是鲨鱼。但是，究竟这都是一条鲨鱼干的，还是另有别的鲨鱼呢？当时，大多数人

---

amputate *v.* 切断；截肢　　　　　　　scour *v.* （彻底地）搜寻，搜查
flesh *n.* 肉体；肉　　　　　　　　　　identify *v.* 辨认

**TOTAL PANIC**

white shark would never swim into an inland creek. The deadly *bull* shark, however, loves *shallow* water. So there were probably several dangerous sharks off the coast of New Jersey that summer. Luckily, though, the attacks stopped after the great white was killed. In time, life went back to normal for people in the area. But residents never again thought of sharks as "harmless."

---

认为所有的袭击事件都是同一条疯狂的鲨鱼所为。现在我们知道，事实很可能不是这样的。大白鲨不会游到内陆的河流中，然而，公牛鲨喜欢在浅水中活动。因此，在那个夏天，很可能有好几条充满危险的鲨鱼游到新泽西近海岸。所幸，在人们杀死那条大白鲨之后，类似的袭击事件停止了。很快，这一地区的人们恢复了正常简单的生活。但是，居民们再也不认为鲨鱼是"与人无害的"了。

---

bull *n.* 公牛 　　　　　　　　　　　　　　　　shallow *adj.* 浅的

# A Sniper in the Tower

The note began, "To whom it may *concern*." On July 31, 1966, Charles Whitman wrote this note as his last message to the world. The 25-year-old University of Texas student knew he did not have long to live. "I am prepared to die," he wrote. He went on to say more. "I *intend* to kill

*On one terrible July afternoon in 1966, the normally peaceful Austin campus of the University of Texas rang out with gunfire. Charles Whitman stood on the observation tower with a loaded rifle and shot at human targets across the entire campus.*

---

## 塔楼枪手

　　1966年一个可怕的下午，素日平静的得克萨斯大学奥斯丁校区里突然枪声大作。查尔斯·惠特曼站在瞭望塔里，端着上好子弹的步枪，疯狂地射击穿梭在校园中的每个人。

　　短签的开头写道"致可能关系到的所有人"。1966年7月31日，查尔斯·惠特曼写下这封短签作为他的绝命书。这个25岁的得克萨斯大学学生知道他不会活很长时间了。他写道"我已经作好了死的准备"。接着，他说了更多东西。"我打算杀死我的妻子。因为我的行为必然会使她万分难

---

concern  v.  涉及；关系到　　　　　　　　　　　intend  v.  打算

TOTAL PANIC

my wife. I don't want her to face the *embarrassment* that my actions will surely cause her."

What actions? Whitman had hinted at the answer four months earlier. He had gone to see psychiatrist Maurice Heatly. Whitman told Dr. Heatly he feared his own "violent impulses." He confessed to beating his wife, Kathy, more than once. Then he said something even scarier. He described his urge to go up to the top of a school tower "with a deer rifle and start shooting people."

Heatly later said that Whitman had been "*oozing* with *hostility*." But Heatly wasn't alarmed. Lots of students, he said, say crazy things. Most of them don't mean it. Heatly told Whitman to come back for another visit. (Whitman never did.) Beyond that, Heatly did nothing.

Who was Charles Whitman? And why was he so angry? Most

---

过，我不想让她面临这种窘境。"

他指的是什么行为呢？早在4个月以前，惠特曼就已经暗示了答案。他去见精神病专家莫里斯·希特雷。惠特曼告诉希特雷医生，他害怕自己的"暴力冲动"。他承认自己曾经不止一次殴打妻子凯西，然后又说了一些更为恐怖的东西。他说自己有一种强烈的欲望，就是爬到学校的塔楼顶部，"手拿一挺狩猎用的步枪，开始向人群射击"。

后来，希特雷说惠特曼那时已经"透露出恶意"。但是希特雷并未警觉起来。他说很多学生都会谈一些疯狂的事情，而他们大多数都不会当真去做。希特雷告诉惠特曼以后再来见一次面。（惠特曼再没来过。）除此之外，希特雷没有采取任何措施。

查尔斯·惠特曼是何许人也？他为什么这么恼怒？多数认识他的人感

---

embarrassment n. 窘迫　　　　　　　　　　　　ooze v. 渗出；流出
hostility n. 敌意

◆ A SNIPER IN THE TOWER

people who knew him had no clue. Whitman kept his anger well hidden. To the outside world, he was an "All-American boy." He was an Eagle Scout at the age of 12. He was an *altar* boy in church. Whitman also had a paper route and played sports. "He was a nice little boy," recalled one neighbor.

As a young adult, Whitman became a Boy Scout leader. The children loved him. "Why, I remember last summer when he had to go away," said one parent. "My son cried because Charlie wouldn't be around."

But there was another Charles Whitman. In his final note, he wrote how he hated his father "with a *mortal* passion." Over the years, he had often seen his father beat his mother. Just recently, Whitman's mother had moved out. When she did, Charles Whitman

---

到大惑不解。惠特曼把自己的这种愤怒情绪掩藏得很深。外面的人认为，他是一个"地道的美国男孩"。他12岁时成为雄鹰童子军的一员。他是教堂里的祭台助手，负责一条发送报纸的路线，并进行各种体育运动。一位邻居回忆说："他是个可爱的小男孩。"

作为一个已经成年了的年轻人，惠特曼成为一位童子军领导人。孩子们都很爱他。一位家长说："嗯，我还记得去年夏天他要离开时，我儿子都哭了，因为查尔斯不会再来了。"

但是，查尔斯·惠特曼还有另外一面。在绝命书中，他写道，他憎恨父亲，对父亲"极端情绪化"。多年以来，他经常看到父亲殴打母亲。就在最近，惠特曼的母亲搬走了。母亲搬家的时候，查尔斯·惠特曼叫来警

---

altar *n.* 祭坛     mortal *adj.* 极端的；致命的

### TOTAL PANIC

called the police to keep watch over her. He feared that his father might show up and get *violent*.

But it was the son, not the father, who turned out to be a killer. On the night of July 31, Whitman went to his mother's apartment. He killed her. Then he added some lines to his note. "I have just killed my mother," he wrote. "If there's a *heaven*, she is going there. If there's not a heaven, she is out of her pain and *misery*. I love my mother with all my heart."

Whitman then returned to his home. He murdered his wife as she lay sleeping. The next day, Whitman took out his *rage* on the rest of the world. He climbed to the top of the University of Texas tower. It was the tallest building in Austin. Dressed as a repairman, Whitman took the elevator to the 27th floor. He had a footlocker with him.

---

察看护她。他担心父亲会突然出现并采取某些暴力行动。

但最终是儿子而不是父亲成了杀人凶手。7月31日夜里，查尔斯来到母亲住的公寓，他杀死了母亲。然后他在绝命书中添了几行字："我刚刚杀死自己的妈妈。如果真的有天堂，她一定会去那儿的，如果没有天堂，她也终于摆脱掉所有的痛苦与不幸了。我太爱我的妈妈了"。

然后惠特曼转身回家。他杀死了熟睡中的妻子。第二天，惠特曼把他的愤怒情绪发泄给全世界的人。他爬到得克萨斯大学塔楼顶部。这个塔楼是全奥斯丁最高的建筑。惠特曼化装成一名修理工，乘电梯到了27楼。他随身带

---

violent  *adj.*  猛烈的；暴力的  
misery  *n.*  痛苦；不幸  

heaven  *n.*  天堂  
rage  *n.*  愤怒

◆ A SNIPER IN THE TOWER

Inside, he had stuffed food, water, knives, guns, and hundreds of *bullets*.

Whitman dragged the footlocker up the last few stairs to the top floor. He planned to go out onto the observation deck. A woman was sitting at a desk next to the door. Her name was Edna Townsley. She never had a chance. Whitman hit her over the head with a rifle butt. Then he shot her and dragged her body behind a sofa. She died a few hours later.

As Whitman *unpacked* his *arsenal*, six people came walking up the stairs. It was a family who just wanted to see the *view*. Whitman heard them coming. Quickly, he grabbed a gun and started shooting. Two of the people fell back down the stairs, dead. Two others were badly wounded. The remaining two tried to help the wounded. Whitman

---

着一个小提箱，里面装满了食物、饮用水、小刀、枪支和数百发子弹。

惠特曼拎着提箱爬上通向顶层的最后几层楼梯。他打算走到瞭望台上。一位妇人正坐在一张挨着门的桌子旁边，她叫埃德娜·汤斯雷。她还没反应过来是怎么回事，惠特曼就用步枪的枪托向她头部猛击过去。然后惠特曼向她开了几枪，并把她拖到一个沙发后面。几小时后，这位妇人就死掉了。

正当惠特曼打开带着的枪支弹药包时，有6个人顺着楼梯走上来。他们是一家人，正想来这里看看风景。惠特曼听到他们走近了，就迅速拿起枪开始射击。有两个人倒在楼梯上，当场死亡，有两个人身受重伤，另外

---

bullet  n. 子弹
arsenal  n. 武器库

unpack  v. 打开包裹
view  n. 风景；视野

**TOTAL PANIC**

then went to the top of the stairs and slammed the door shut.

It was 11:48 A.M. when Whitman got out onto the observation deck. The walkway was six feet wide and went all the way around the tower. Through the *scope* on his rifle, Whitman could see the whole *campus*. With a cool and deadly aim, he opened fire. He moved around the tower, shooting in all directions. Clearly, he wanted to kill people—lots of people.

At first, no one down below knew what the odd puffs of smoke from the tower meant. Then people started falling. Still, it took a few moments for others to understand that there was a sniper on the tower.

Norma Barger heard loud noises and looked out her window. She saw six bodies lying on the ground. She thought it was a student

---

两个人去抢救伤者。惠特曼走到楼顶，然后把那扇门用力关上。

中午11时48分，惠特曼走上瞭望台。步道有6英尺宽，环绕着塔楼。惠特曼可以看到整个校园都处在他步枪的射程内。满怀冷酷和绝望，他开火了。他在塔楼上走来走去，把子弹射向四面八方。显然，他要杀人——杀很多人。

起初，下面没有人知道塔楼上喷出的阵阵烟尘意味着什么。然后，人们开始纷纷倒地。又过了一会儿，人们才意识到塔楼上有一名狙击手。

诺玛·巴格尔听到了喧嚷声，于是她往窗外望去。她看到有6个人倒在地上，以为这是学生们搞的恶作剧。"我还以为这6个人会站起来，嬉笑

---

scope *n.* 视野；范围　　　　　　　　　　　　campus *n.* 校园

◆ A SNIPER IN THE TOWER

*prank*. "I expected the six to get up and walk away laughing." Then she saw the blood. Only then did Barger realize it was no joke.

Pat Sonntag was *strolling* across the lawn with Claudia Rutt. The two were holding hands. Suddenly, Claudia *crumpled* to the ground. "Help me," she cried out. As Pat bent over to see what was wrong with her, the *sniper* fired another bullet. Pat collapsed over Claudia's body. Both were mortally wounded.

Robert Boyer was shot and killed on his way to lunch. Thomas Karr had spent all night studying for a big test. He was headed home for a short nap when Whitman gunned him down. Thomas Aston was walking on the roof of a nearby building. Whitman killed him too. Roy Dell Schmidt, who was three blocks away, heard the shooting,

---

着走开呢。"然后她看见他们流血了，此时她才意识到这并非玩笑。

派特·森特格当时正与克劳迪娅·拉特手牵着手在草坪上漫步。突然，克劳迪娅瘫倒在地。她高喊："救命啊！"派特俯下身去看她这究竟是怎么了，这时，狙击手射出另一发子弹。派特倒在克劳迪娅身上。两个人都受了致命的枪伤。

罗伯特·波义尔也被射中了，死在去吃午饭的路上。托马斯·卡尔为了准备一次大型考试学了一个通宵，正要回家小睡片刻。就在这时，惠特曼向他开火，他倒在了地上。托马斯·阿斯顿正往附近一栋楼的楼顶爬去。惠特曼把他也杀死了。罗伊·戴尔·施密特此时正在3个街区以外。

---

prank *n.* 恶作剧
crumple *v.* 瘫倒

stroll *v.* 漫步；闲逛
sniper *n.* 狙击兵

# TOTAL PANIC

then *clutched* his chest and fell dead. "He told me we were out of range," said a man who had been standing next to him.

The police soon arrived. One of the first was Officer Billy Speed. He took cover behind some stone *columns*. But the sniper saw a *slight* opening between the columns. He killed Speed with one bullet. Soon many other officers arrived. They poured heavy fire at the tower. That forced Whitman to keep his head down. Still, he could fire through the drain openings around the base of the tower. So he was able to keep up his *deadly* fire. Before long the campus was littered with the dead and wounded.

During Whitman's stay in the tower, he killed 13 people. He wounded 31 others. One victim was Claire Wilson, who was eight

---

他听到了枪声，一把抓住胸口，卧倒在地。当时站在他旁边的一位男子说道："他告诉我，我们在射程之外。"

警察很快赶到现场。最先到达者之一是警官比利·斯皮特。他隐蔽在几个石柱后面，但狙击手还是看到了石柱之间的一个细缝，用一发子弹结束了斯皮特的性命。没多久，很多警官都赶到了。他们向塔楼猛烈地开火，惠特曼不得不把头低下去。但他可以通过塔基周围的排水口向外射击，所以还是保持着他那足以致命的火力。不久，校园里到处都是死伤者。

惠特曼在塔里的这段时间内共枪杀了13人，击伤31人。克莱尔·威尔逊是受害者之一，当时她已经怀有8个月的身孕。克莱尔活了下来，但

---

clutch  v.  抓住  
slight  adj.  细长的；轻微的

column  n.  圆柱  
deadly  adj.  致命的

◆ A SNIPER IN THE TOWER

months *pregnant*. Claire survived, but her baby did not.

Whitman's reign of terror lasted more than an hour and a half. No one could kill him from the ground. At last, four men decided to go into the building, hoping to get him from in there. The men were led by Romero Martinez, an *off-duty* police officer. They took the elevator to the 27th floor. Then they walked up the stairs past the spot where the first four people had been shot. The men opened the door and crept out onto the observation deck. Martinez inched his way in one direction. A man named Allen Crum went the other way. Crum fired some shots to distract Whitman. It worked. Martinez caught Whitman by surprise and shot him dead.

At last the nightmare was over. The terror *subsided*. But the *grief* lasted much longer. For the families of the victims, nothing would ever be the same again.

---

是腹中的婴儿没有保住。

惠特曼控制的令人恐怖的局面超过一个半小时。没有人能从地面上把他击毙。最后，4名男子决定进入塔楼，希望能在里面把他捉住。这些人由一个不当班的警官罗莫罗·马丁内斯带领，乘坐电梯上到27楼。然后他们顺着楼梯往上爬，经过最开始有4个人被射中的那个地方。几个人打开那扇门，蹑手蹑脚地走到瞭望台上。马丁内斯朝着一个方向慢慢移动，另一名叫做艾伦·克拉姆的男子朝与他相反的方向挪动过去。为了转移惠特曼的视线，克拉姆开了几枪。这一招很管用。马丁内斯出其不意地抓住了惠特曼，并将他当场击毙。

最后，噩梦终于结束了，人们的恐怖情绪慢慢平息下去。但是悲伤的气氛却持续了更长时间。对于受害者的家人，整个世界变得完全不同了。

---

pregnant *adj.* 怀孕的；怀胎的
subside *v.* 平息

off-duty *adj.* 不当班的；下了班的
grief *n.* 悲痛；忧伤

## TOTAL PANIC

**9**

# The Night the Dam Let Go

Tony Harnischfeger did not like what he was seeing. The St. Francis Dam was *discharging* "dirty" water. As *dam* keeper, Harnischfeger knew the water should be clear. So he asked William Mulholland, the builder of the dam, to check it out. Mulholland

*The St. Francis Dam, which supplied water to Los Angeles, unexpectedly let go on the night of March 12, 1928. When the dam broke, 12 billion gallons of water spilled down the canyon below, killing at least 450 sleeping people.*

---

## 大坝崩塌

负责向洛杉矶市供水的圣弗朗西斯大坝，于1928年3月12日夜间，出乎意料地崩塌了。坝体破裂后，120亿加仑洪水泄入下游的峡谷之中，造成至少450个正在熟睡的人死亡。

托尼·哈尼施芬格不愿见到眼前的一切。圣弗朗西斯大坝正在向下游倾泻着"肮脏的"水流。作为大坝的管理者，哈尼施芬格知道，水流应该是清澈的。因此他让大坝的建造者威廉·缪忽兰去检查一下。缪忽兰对大

---

discharge *v.* 排放；流出      dam *n.* 大坝

◆ THE NIGHT THE DAM LET GO

*inspected* the dam. He pronounced it sound. He said there was no need to worry.

Later that same day, March 12, 1928, Bill Riley stopped by the dam. He, his wife Abigail, and their two daughters wanted to see the great St. Francis Dam. People called it an engineering *marvel*. Its walls were 200 feet high. They held back 12 billion gallons of water. The dam was a key source of water for the city of Los Angeles, 50 miles to the south.

Like Harnischfeger, Riley saw something he did not like. Water was *seeping* into the rocky soil at the foot of the dam. "This dam could go!" he warned his wife.

She just laughed at him. "Don't be *silly*," she said. "Those people wouldn't have built a dam that weak." Still, Riley didn't want to take

---

坝视察一番后，断定坝体是完好的。他说没有担心的必要。

1928年3月12日，在这一天的傍晚，比尔·瑞里来到大坝前。他本人、妻子阿比盖尔和他的两个女儿想来参观一下这座雄伟的圣弗朗西斯大坝。人们把它称作工程奇迹。坝堤高达200英尺，里面蓄积了120亿加仑的水量。这座大坝在洛杉矶以南50英里，是这座城市的重要水源。

和哈尼施芬格一样，瑞里也目睹了一些他不愿意看到的东西。有水渗进大坝底部坚实的土壤里。他向妻子警告说："大坝就要塌了！"

妻子马上就讥笑他："别傻了，那些人不会修筑一个那么脆弱的大坝

---

inspect *v.* 检阅；视察
seep *v.* 渗出；漏

marvel *n.* 奇迹
silly *adj.* 愚蠢的；糊涂的

**TOTAL PANIC**

any chances. He told his family to get back into the truck. Then he floored the gas *pedal*. "Bill broke every speed limit to get away," his wife said later.

Maybe Bill Riley just made a lucky guess. But he was right on the money. At 11:57 that evening, the dam gave way. First one side *collapsed*. Then the other side went. Finally the middle fell too. Twelve billion gallons of raging water poured over the *crumbling* walls of the dam. It was enough to form a wave 75 feet high.

The deadly wave roared down the San Francisquito Canyon. It *wiped out* more than 1,200 ranch houses that dotted the canyon. One writer wrote that homes were "crushed like egg shells." The water ripped up trees and washed away bridges. It also knocked out power lines and flooded all the towns in the valley.

---

的。"但瑞里还是不想再耽搁了。他告诉家人回到卡车里，然后他踩下了油门。他的妻子后来说："比尔以最快的速度逃离了那里。"

也许比尔·瑞里只是做了一个幸运的猜测而已，但是他的决定是正确的。当晚11时57分，大坝垮掉了。先是一边倒塌，然后是另一边，最后连中间的都倒掉了。120万加仑的水从破碎的坝堤上面咆哮着倾泻下来，形成的狂涛能达到75英尺高。

致命的波涛顺着圣弗朗西斯科峡谷狂奔而下，吞没了散布在峡谷中的超过1200间农舍。一位作家形容这些房子"像蛋壳碎掉了一样"。大水把树木连根拔起，桥梁被冲毁，输电线被冲断，淹没了峡谷里的所有城镇。

---

pedal *n.* 踏板；脚蹬  
crumble *v.* 破碎；成碎屑  

collapse *v.* 倒塌  
wipe out 消灭；彻底摧毁

◆ THE NIGHT THE DAM LET GO

Most inhabitants of the canyon were asleep when the dam broke. They had little chance to survive. The water *engulfed* many people in their beds. Some, however, heard the roar of the water as it approached. It sounded like a runaway *freight* train. People who heard it threw on their shoes and *dashed* for higher ground. Some made it; others did not.

John Haskell was one who heard the wild water coming. He rushed to warn his family, screaming, "The dam's gone out! We've got to find Clara and Oscar!" But it was too late. His aunt Clara Willmont was lost in the flood. Somehow his uncle Oscar survived. But the poor man was *overcome* with grief. The loss of his wife and other family members was more than he could take. A short time later, Oscar, too, died.

---

大坝崩塌时峡谷中的大多数居民正在熟睡，他们生还的可能性非常小。大水即将吞没他们时，很多人还在床上。但还是有一些人听到了洪水接近时发出的咆哮声，就像是一列失控的载货列车。听到水声的人们急忙穿上鞋逃到高处。有些人做到了，但有些人没有做到。

有人听到了疯狂的洪流到来的声音，约翰·海斯克就是其中之一。他急忙去警告家人。他大喊道："大坝垮了！我们得赶快去找克莱拉和奥斯卡！"但为时已晚。他的婶婶克莱拉·威蒙特已经被洪水冲走了，不知何故，他的叔叔奥斯卡幸存下来。但是这个可怜的人已经悲痛欲绝，他无法承受失去妻子和其他亲人的痛苦。不久之后，奥斯卡也死了。

---

engulf *v.* 吞没  
dash *v.* 猛冲  

freight *n.* 货运  
overcome *v.* 战胜；克服

### TOTAL PANIC

Some people survived by grabbing a piece of *debris* and riding with the flow of water. Eighty-year-old C. H. Hunick lived in a *ranch* house a mile and a half from the dam. "When the water hit it, the house crumbled as though it were built of cards," he later *recalled*. Hunick couldn't see anything in the darkness. But he managed to reach out and grab onto something.

It turned out to be a *chunk* of his own roof. "Down, down with the current we went," he said. "I kept saying to myself every second was my last. I knew that I could not last long... My strength was going fast, but I hung on." Then, out of the darkness, an arm reached out and seized him.

"Is that you, Dad?" a voice shouted. It was Hunick's own son.

---

有些人抓住了一些一鳞半爪的东西，从洪流中脱身而出，得以生还。80岁的C. H. 汉尼克住在大坝外一英里半地的一间农舍里。他后来回忆道："洪水袭来的时候，房子被完全冲垮了，就像是纸糊的一样。"黑暗之中，汉尼克什么都看不见。但最终他还是费了很大力气逃了出来，伸手抓住了什么东西。

其实他抓住的是自家房顶的一部分。他说："我们顺着水流漂啊，漂啊，我每时每刻都对自己说，就要完蛋了。我知道自己坚持不了多久了……我的体力快速地消耗着，但我一直坚持着。"后来，透过黑暗，一只臂膀伸了过来，抓住了他。

一个声音高叫道："是你吗，爸爸？"原来这是汉尼克的亲生儿子。

---

debris *n.* 残骸；碎片  
recall *v.* 回忆  

ranch *n.* 大农场；大牧场  
chunk *n.* 块

◆ THE NIGHT THE DAM LET GO

The son pulled Hunick over onto the *plank* he was floating on. Later, the two men were rescued and taken to a hospital. There, C. H. Hunick began asking about his other two sons. Sadly, the doctors had to tell him that both had *perished* earlier that night in the flood.

Ann Holzcloth's home was also destroyed by the raging water. She was in bed with her baby when the wave struck. "I clutched him tight as we were swept out on the water in the dark," she said. She managed to grab a piece of floating *lumber* with one hand. "With my other arm, I held the baby out of the water the best I could." They soon hit a powerful *whirlpool*, however, and the force of the water ripped the baby from her grasp. The violent wave tossed Holzcloth up onto dry land. But it carried her son away. "Why did I have to live?" she wept.

---

儿子把汉尼克拖到自己漂浮着的木板上。后来，两个人被搭救上来并送往医院。在医院里，C. H. 汉尼克开始询问他另外两个儿子的情况。医生很沉痛地告诉他，当晚，他那两个儿子已经在洪水中被淹死了。

安·霍兹克劳斯的家也被汹涌而来的大水冲毁了。正当她和孩子躺在床上的时候，洪水冲了进来。她说："我紧紧地抓住他，在黑暗中，大水把我们冲走了。"她用一只手费力地抓住一块漂浮着的木头。另一只胳膊尽力把孩子托出水面。很快，他们遇到一个强大的漩涡。水流的力量把孩子从她手中冲开。猛烈的波涛把霍兹克劳斯冲上一片旱地，但是把他的儿子卷走了。她哭着说："我自己活着还有什么意思啊？"

---

plank *n.* 厚板  
lumber *n.* 木材；木料

perish *v.* 死亡；毁灭  
whirlpool *n.* 漩涡

TOTAL PANIC

Many other people died that awful night. Rescue workers found heartbreaking evidence of the victims' final *frantic* moments. Most people died in their nightclothes. One little girl was wearing just one untied shoe. Others had had their clothing ripped off by the rushing water.

The death toll was set at 450. But the true count was probably much higher. Professor Doyce B. Nunis thinks it was more like 600. Nunis points out that many bodies "were washed into the ocean." Also, there were a number of migrant workers in the region. As Nunis notes, many of them "were never accounted for."

What caused the dam to break? The blame has always been pinned on William Mulholland. He was supposed to have built an "impregnable" *masterpiece*. Instead, his dam crumbled after just two

---

在那个可怕的深夜，其他很多人都遇难了。营救人员发现了受害者在最后那个疯狂的时刻心情极度悲痛的证据。大多数人遇难时还穿着睡衣。有个小姑娘还穿者一只没系带的鞋，其他人身上穿的衣服都被急流冲走了。

最后确定的死亡人数为450人，但是实际的数字可能要高得多。道斯·B·纳尼斯教授认为实际死亡人数要超过六百人。纳尼斯指出，许多尸体"已经被冲到海洋里去了"。另外，这一地区还有许多流动工人。正如纳尼斯所说，他们当中的很多人"没有被统计在内"。

引发大坝崩塌的原因究竟是什么呢？人们总是将其归罪于威廉·缪忽兰身上。人们以为他建造出了一件"固若金汤"的杰作，结果他的这座大

---

frantic  *adj.*  疯狂的        masterpiece  *n.*  杰作

◆ THE NIGHT THE DAM LET GO

years. Some people claimed it had not been properly anchored in bedrock. They said that underground water had seeped into the dam and *weakened* it.

Before the dam's *collapse*, Mulholland was a local hero. He was the one who had used *aqueducts* and dams to bring water to parched Los Angeles. After the dam's collapse, however, people hated him. One woman hammered a sign into the front yard of her mud-filled home. The sign read: KILL MULHOLLAND.

Mulholland bravely took responsibility for the disaster. "Don't blame anyone else," he said. "You just fasten it on me. If there is an error of human judgment, I was the human."

But was he really to blame? A 1995 book written by engineer J. David Rogers says no. According to Rogers, the dam was built on

坝建成仅两年就倒塌了。有些人认为坝体没有完全固定在岩基之上。他们说是地下水渗进了坝体由此导致坝体变得脆弱。

大坝倒塌之前，缪忽兰是当地人心目中的英雄，他用水渠和大坝给干渴的洛杉矶市带来甘泉。然而，大坝倒塌之后，当地人就恨上他了。一位妇人在她满是泥泞的住处的前院里钉起一块标语牌，上面写着：处死缪忽兰。

缪忽兰勇敢地承担了对这次灾难的责任。他说："不要谴责其他人了，过错由我一人承担。如果说存在人为过失的话，我就是那个人。"

但是，他确实应该被谴责吗？工程师J. 大卫·罗杰斯1995年写的一本书中否定了这种看法。根据罗杰斯所述，大坝是在远古崩塌的碎石基础

weaken *v.* 变弱  
aqueduct *n.* 沟渠；导水管

collapse *n.* 倒塌

## TOTAL PANIC

top of rubble from an ancient *landslide*. Mulholland had no way of knowing that. The rubble was too far underground to be detected. But the weight of the dam caused the *rubble* to shift. That, in turn, caused the dam to give way.

If Rogers is right, the bursting of the St. Francis Dam was not Mulholland's fault. But that is small comfort for families of the victims. For them, the night the dam broke would always be the worst night of their lives.

---

上建造起来的。缪忽兰无法知道这一情况。碎石在地下极深处，不可能被探测到。但坝体的重量引起碎石层的移动，地层的逐渐移动最终导致大坝崩塌。

　　如果罗杰斯的说法是正确的，圣弗朗西斯大坝的倒塌就不是缪忽兰的过错了。但是这并未给受害的家庭带来多少安慰。对他们来说，大坝崩塌之夜将是他们这一生中最糟糕的夜晚。

---

landslide  n.  山崩　　　　　　　　　　　　　　　　rubble  n.  碎石

# Flood in Mozambique

They never saw it coming. "The water came so quickly," said one woman. "We were running, there was no time to get anything but the chicken. It was coming higher in a great rush, and all we could do was climb a tree."

In February 2000 a huge *tropical*

When floodwater covered their homes, many frightened families ran up to rooftops or climbed into the upper branches of tall trees. For days they clung to their uncomfortable perches waiting for rescue.

## 莫桑比克洪灾

洪水淹没房屋时，受到惊吓的人们跑上屋顶，或者爬到大树高处的枝桠上面。一连好几天，他们困守在那个地方，等待救援。

他们从未见过这么大的洪水。一位妇人说："洪水来得太快了，我们赶紧跑，除了几只鸡，我们没时间带别的东西。水面越来越高，涨得越来越快，我们只能往树上爬。"

2000年2月，一次极为猛烈的热带风暴袭击了莫桑比克这个非洲国家。大雨

---

tropical  *adj.*  热带的

### TOTAL PANIC

storm hit the African nation of Mozambique. Heavy rain caused rivers to pour over their banks. Dams *overflowed*. The Limpopo River had been little more than a *trickle*. Suddenly it was two miles wide. The flood swept up homes, even whole villages. Hundreds of people drowned. Nearly a million were left homeless. "It's like the gods have abandoned us," said one man. "We can't believe this is happening to our country."

The woman with the chicken was among the lucky ones. When the flood hit her village, some people panicked and just ran. But she climbed a tree with her six-month-old baby *strapped* to her back. Some of her neighbors did the same. As they clung to the branches, they watched the brown floodwater of the Limpopo River raging below them. "I saw people drowning," said the woman. "We were relieved to [get] to the tree. But it was scary with all the insects and no food or sleep. I only held on because of my baby."

---

导致河水溢出堤岸，大坝也被淹没了。原本几乎干涸的林波河，突然间水面阔达两英里。民房，甚至整个村庄都被洪水冲毁。数百人被淹死，近一百万人无家可归。一名男子说："上帝好像是抛弃了我们。真不敢相信我的家乡会出这种事。"

　　带出了几只鸡的那位妇人是个幸运儿。洪水到达她所在的村庄时，有些人惊慌失措，赶快逃跑了。但是她背着6个月大的孩子爬上一棵树。有几个邻居也是这么做的。他们抓住树枝，看着林波河里浑黑的洪水从身下咆哮而过。这位妇人说："我看到有人淹死了。我们爬上树，这才捡了一条命。但是小昆虫满天飞，我们没有食物，没办法睡觉，这真是太可怕了。就是因为孩子，我才挺了过来。"

---

overflow　*v.*　漫出；溢出　　　　　　　　　trickle　*n.*　细流；涓流
strap　*v.*　用带捆绑

◆ FLOOD IN MOZAMBIQUE

Holding on wasn't easy. If any of the people in the trees fell asleep, they might fall out and drown. None of them had more to eat than a piece of bread or an ear of corn. Some had nothing at all. As the hours passed, their hunger grew. So did their weariness. But still they hung on. Hour after hour, day after day, they clung to the trees and prayed that rescuers would come.

During the day the temperature often rose to 100 degrees or more. But the nights were even worse. That was when the *mosquitoes* came out. Also, other creatures had fled to the trees to escape the flood. So people had to share their haven with stinging ants, rats, and snakes. "It was like another world—just the water *beneath* us and the sky above," said one woman.

Even before the flood hit, the people in Mozambique had difficult lives. They are among the poorest people in the world. The *average* person makes less than $150 per year. That is why the woman

---

能坚持下来真是不容易。如果树上的人睡着了，他们就会掉下来淹死。他们每个人最多也就是吃一片面包或者一穗谷子而已，有人什么也吃不到。时间一点一点地过去了，他们更加饥饿，因此更加疲惫不堪，但他们仍旧坚持着。几个小时过去了，几天过去了，他们还是吊在树上，祈祷有人来救他们。

那段时间，白天的气温经常达到100华氏度甚至更高。但是夜里情况更加糟糕，因为蚊子出来活动了。另外，其他动物也为躲避洪水而逃到树上。因此，灾民不得不与蜇人的蚂蚁、老鼠、蛇共享他们的天地。一位妇人说："那就好像是另外一个世界——脚下只有洪水，头顶只有天空。"

在洪水袭来之前，莫桑比克人的生活就已经很艰难了。他们是世界上最贫穷的一群人，每人的年均收入不到一百五十美元。这就是那位妇人要拼命

---

mosquito *n.* 蚊子  beneath *prep.* 在……之下
average *adj.* 普通的；平常的

## TOTAL PANIC

bothered to take the chicken. It was her sole *possession*. The other villagers were just as poor. Because they had no radios, they got no warning about the flood. Also, none of these people had cars or trucks. They couldn't drive to higher and drier land. The woman who took the chicken had never been inside a car. So when the floodwater came, the people's only hope was to climb a tall tree or a rooftop.

But in a poor country *devastated* by floodwater, who was left to rescue survivors? Mozambique did not have the skilled people and equipment to help the victims. "We cannot do this alone," said the president. "The damage is massive and we need help fast."

Yet other countries acted slowly. Perhaps they did not know how bad the flood really was. In any case, the only nation that rushed to help was South Africa. That country, too, had been hit by the flood, but not as badly. It sent 12 helicopters to lift people out of trees and

---

带出几只鸡的原因，那是她唯一的家当。其他村民同样的贫穷。因为没有收音机，所以他们没有得到发洪水的警报。而且，他们都没有小汽车或者卡车，不可能躲到地势更高，更加干燥的地方。带出几只鸡的那位妇人从来没坐过小汽车。所以洪水来临时，人们唯一的希望就是能够爬到大树或者房顶上去。

在一个遭到洪灾蹂躏的贫穷国家里，又有谁能去营救幸存者呢？莫桑比克没有训练有素的人员和精良的装备去营救那些受难者。总统说："我们自己做不到这一点。受灾情况太惨重了，我们急需帮助。"

其他国家行动迟缓，可能是因为他们并不清楚这次洪灾有多么严重。不管怎么说，提供紧急救援的只有一个国家，那就是南非。它也遭到这次洪灾的袭击，但是没有那么严重。南非派出12架直升机，把灾民从树上和

---

possession  *n.*  财产；所有物                    devastate  *v.*  破坏；蹂躏

◆ FLOOD IN MOZAMBIQUE

off rooftops.

It was tough work. The flooded area was vast and it was hard to see people in the trees. Often, pilots had to use the wind caused by the helicopters' *blades* to flatten out tree leaves a bit. Only then could pilots see if there were people in a tree to rescue. The pilots flew day after day with little sleep. They did this for more than two weeks. In the end, they saved nearly 14,000 people. "They are the real heroes," said one official.

Of all the survivors, it was Sophia Pedro whose story *captured* the world's attention. Like so many others, she and her family are poor. All they owned were 10 pigs and 10 chickens. They lived in a grass hut in a rural village. "We did not have [the] money for bricks," said her husband.

Sophia was nine months pregnant when the flood hit. She, her husband, and their two children were at home at the time. The

---

屋顶救出来。

这是一项艰苦的工作。受灾面积非常大，看清树上的人非常困难。飞行员经常需要用直升机桨叶吹出的风将树叶微微吹开，这样才能看清树上究竟有没有需要营救的人。飞行员们持续进行这项工作超过两周时间，几乎很少睡觉，最后共救出近一万四千人。一位官员说："他们是真正的英雄。"

生还者中，索菲娅·彼得的经历引起了全世界的关注。和很多人一样，她和她的家人都非常贫穷。他们只有10头猪，10只鸡。他们住在乡间的一座小草屋里。她的丈夫说："我们没钱买砖。"

洪水到来时，索菲娅已有9个月身孕。她和丈夫，还有两个孩子当时

---

blade *n.* 桨叶　　　　　　　　　　　capture *v.* 引起（注意）

## TOTAL PANIC

water rose so fast they barely got out in time. They fled with just the clothes on their backs. Luckily they managed to *scramble* up into a tree. But they hadn't had time to take any food with them. So they had nothing to eat. The only water they had to drink was the muddy water below. For four days they stayed in the tree, clinging to life.

Then, on the fourth day, two miracles occurred. First, Sophia gave birth to a baby girl. Somehow, she managed to hang onto a branch during her labor pains. Second, the family was saved by a helicopter. Moments after the baby's birth, a *medic* was lowered down to the tree. There he cut the baby's cord and comforted Sophia. "We spotted her just in time," he said. "We then *hoisted* mother and child onto the helicopter." The drama was caught by a TV crew and broadcast around the world. Many people saw the birth as a ray of hope in a sea of misery.

Despite their *ordeal*, Sophia and her baby, named Rositha, were

---

正在屋里。水位上涨太快，他们几乎没有时间跑出去，他们只穿了件背心就逃出屋去。幸运的是他们想方设法爬到一棵树上，但是根本没时间把食品带出来。因此他们什么吃的都没有。他们只能喝下面浑浑的洪水。他们在树上停留四天之久，坚持着活了下来。

然后，就在第四天，发生了两个奇迹。首先，索菲娅生出一个女孩。不知为什么，在产前阵痛时她竟然还能够抓住树枝，还有，他们一家人终于被直升机救出来了。孩子出生不久，医生就降落到树上，他切断了婴儿的脐带，并且安抚索菲娅。他说："我们及时发现了她。然后，我们把母子抬进直升飞机。"这个场景被电视台的工作人员拍摄下来，并向全世界进行了播放。人们把孩子的出生当成是悲痛海洋中的一缕希望之光。

尽管倍受折磨，索菲娅和她孩子罗西塔身体状况良好。她说："非常

---

scramble  *v.*  爬行  
hoist  *v.*  使升起  

medic  *n.*  医生；医师  
ordeal  *n.*  折磨

◆ FLOOD IN MOZAMBIQUE

in good shape. "We are very happy to have been *rescued*," she said. "We have no problem."

But what kind of future would Rositha have? After the rescue, her father said, "We have nothing. We had our last meal four days ago. Our village is all gone."

Soon the leader of Mozambique stepped in to help. The *president* promised that the family would get a better place to live and food to eat. He also said the government would pay for Rositha's schooling. The president said the girl was a symbol of the suffering of all children in the nation. So although Rositha's life started on a *shaky* note, it seemed she would have a *decent* chance for a good life.

---

高兴，我们得救了，我们没事儿。"

但是罗西塔会面临一个怎样的未来呢？得救之后，她爸爸说："我们一无所有。我们最后一口饭是4天前吃的，我们的村子不在了。"

很快，莫桑比克的领导人就介入救援行动。总统许诺，这一家人会得到更好的住处，并得到充足的食物，还说政府会为罗西塔支付学费。总统说，这个女孩是整个国家所有受灾儿童的一个象征。因此，尽管罗西塔的生命有一个悲惨的开端，但是看起来她的未来已充满希望。

---

rescue *v.* 救援；营救  
shaky *adj.* 摇晃的；不可靠的

president *n.* 总统  
decent *adj.* 得体的；相当好的

TOTAL PANIC

# 11

# Tragedy in the Baltic Sea

It was just after midnight on the ferryboat Estonia. Andrus Maidre awoke with a start. From below his *cabin* came loud crashing sounds. Dozens of cars and trucks were sliding back and forth, *smashing* into each other. As 19-year-old Maidre crawled up the *tilting* stairway

*Finnish military personnel load the coffin of a shipwreck victim onto a ferryboat on the Baltic Sea. The calm waters give no hint of the violence of the storm that struck only days earlier. This victim and 858 others lost their lives when the ferry Estonia sank during a storm.*

## 波罗的海悲歌

芬兰军人抬着海难中一名遇难者的棺木走到波罗的海的一艘渡轮上。在平静的海面上，人们根本看不到几天前发生的风暴的任何痕迹。在这场风暴中，爱沙尼亚号渡轮沉没。这名遇难者，还有另外858人，就在这次事故中失去了生命。

在午夜刚过的爱沙尼亚号渡轮上，安德鲁斯·梅卓被惊醒了。从他所在船舱的下面发出剧烈的撞击声。许多小汽车，还有卡车，来回地滑动，相互之间猛烈地碰撞着。当19岁的梅卓顺着斜梯爬到上层甲板时，他才意

cabin *n.* 船舱　　　　　　　　　　　　　　　　　　　smash *v.* 猛撞
tilt *v.* 倾斜

◆ TRAGEDY IN THE BALTIC SEA

to the upper deck, he realized what was happening. The ferryboat was sinking.

The Estonia was a popular ship. It was known for its *restaurants* and shops. It had an indoor swimming pool and a children's playroom. And it had a live band for dancing. In short, sailing on the Estonia was a fun way to cross the Baltic Sea.

On September 27, 1994, the ship sailed from Tallinn, Estonia. It was headed for Stockholm, Sweden. There were 996 people on board. Many were Swedish tourists. For them, the 230-mile trip was a pleasure *cruise*. The forecast called for high winds and *rough* seas. But no one seemed worried. Such conditions were normal at that time of the year. Besides, the Estonia was a big ship. It was more than 500 feet long and weighed more than 15,000 tons. It looked as though it could *handle* any kind of bad weather that came its way.

---

识到发生了什么事情：渡轮正在下沉。

爱沙尼亚号是一艘很受乘客喜爱的轮船。它以上面的餐厅和商店而出名，里面有室内游泳场，儿童游戏厅，还有一支活跃的乐队可以陪伴着起舞的人们。乘坐爱沙尼亚号航行对人们来说就是在波罗的海上的一段美妙旅途。

1994年9月27日，轮船从爱沙尼亚的塔林启航，驶向瑞典的斯德哥尔摩。船上共有996人，其中有很多瑞典的旅游者。对他们来说，这段230英里的旅程是一次令人愉快的航行经历。天气预报说海面上风高浪急，但似乎没有人担心这一点。一年中这样的状况是很平常的。另外，爱沙尼亚号是一艘大轮船，长达五百多英尺，重量超过15,000吨，看上去可以应对航程中出现的任何恶劣天气。

---

restaurant *n.* 餐厅
rough *adj.* 粗野的；艰苦的

cruise *n.* 航行
handle *v.* 处理

**TOTAL PANIC**

By 8:30 that night, the Baltic Sea had turned nasty. Twenty-foot waves battered the ferry. The ship rolled from side to side. The band decided to call it quits early. The sea was getting too rough for dancing. Most of the passengers went to their cabins. By midnight, almost everyone was asleep. Up to that point, it had been just a very *turbulent* night.

But then things turned deadly. The storm grew really violent, with waves swelling to more than 30 feet high. Somehow, the front *cargo* door became ripped open. At 12:10 A.M., a member of the crew glanced up at his TV monitor. He noticed water in the car deck. He thought it was rain coming in. So he ordered the *bilge* pumps turned on.

But the pumps did no good. The water was not simply the result of rain. The sea itself was pouring into the car deck through the

---

当晚8:30，波罗的海开始发威，20英尺高的海浪猛扑渡轮，船体开始晃来晃去，乐队决定早早收场，海面波涛汹涌，船上已经不能跳舞了，大多数乘客回到了船舱。午夜时分，大多数人已经熟睡了。实事求是地说，那真是一个极为动荡的夜晚。

但是随后情况变得极为可怕。风暴变得异常猛烈，浪高涨到30英尺以上，前面的舱门已被撕开。中午12:10，一位船员朝上看了一眼他的电视监控器。他注意到载车甲板上面有积水，以为是雨水进来了，于是打开了船底排水泵。

但是那些泵是不管用的。这些水不仅仅是下雨造成的，海水正通过破

---

turbulent *adj.* 动荡的　　　　　　　　　　　cargo *n.* 货物；货船
bilge *n.* 船底（弯曲部）

◆ TRAGEDY IN THE BALTIC SEA

broken cargo door. Tons of water *sloshed* from side to side in the car deck. The crew soon realized what was happening. But there was little they could do. By 12:24 A.M., they knew all hope was lost. The message went out: "*Mayday*, Estonia. We are sinking."

By that time, the ship was leaning sharply to the left. Cars and trucks began to bang into each other. As the noise woke the passengers, fear and *confusion* swept through the ship. People rushed around, screaming for help. Some wore only their *pajamas*. Others wore nothing. Carl Ovberg later recalled what he saw. "Children and women were running in panic," he said. "Many fell and slid headlong into the walls. You couldn't help them. The boat was swinging and you could hardly manage to stay on your own feet."

Andrus Maidre said, "Some old people had already given up hope. They were just sitting there crying." Maidre added, "I also stepped over

损的货舱门向载车甲板内倾泻，成吨的水在上面四散喷溅。船员们马上意识到发生了什么事情，但是他们也无能为力。中午12:24，他们知道已经没什么希望了。通讯信号发了出去："爱沙尼亚号紧急求救！我们正在下沉。"

此时，船体已经急剧向左倾斜。小汽车和卡车开始相互碰撞，刺耳的声音惊醒了乘客，惊慌和混乱传遍整艘轮船。人们四散奔逃，尖声呼救。有些人身上只穿了件睡衣，有些人什么都没穿。卡尔·欧博格后来回忆起他所看到的景象。他说："孩子和妇女们慌张逃命，很多人掉下床，大头朝下滑到墙上，你根本帮不上忙。船晃来晃去，你甚至站都站不稳。"

安德鲁斯·梅卓说："很多老人已经彻底绝望了，只是坐在那儿

slosh *v.* 泼溅  
confusion *n.* 混乱  

mayday *n.* 求救信号  
pajamas *n.* 睡衣

**TOTAL PANIC**

children who were *wailing* and holding on to the railing."

The Estonia had plenty of life rafts. And it had all the life jackets people needed. But the safety equipment did little good. The ship sank too fast for an orderly rescue. In just 35 minutes, it was gone. For the most part, passengers had to look out for themselves. There was no attempt to save the women and children first. "It was the law of the jungle," said Kent Harstedt. "A woman had broken her legs and begged others to give her a life jacket." No one did.

But there was some *heroism* too. One group of Swedes formed a human chain. They threw life jackets to people who had fallen into the sea without one. One man jumped into the water. He swam to one of the life rafts and climbed aboard. Struggling bravely, he pulled others up onto the raft. But, sadly, not everyone made it. "There was an Estonian girl," he later recalled. "I tried to hold on to her, but my

---

哭。"他又说："我从号啕大哭的孩子身边走过去，抓住了扶手。"

爱沙尼亚号上有许多救生筏，也有足够所有人用的救生衣，但是安全装置运转得不够好。船体下沉得太快，无法组织有秩序的救援行动。仅仅35分钟，这艘船就沉没了。乘客们最多也只能是各自保重了。开始没有人想着去救妇女和儿童，肯特·哈特得说："现在是生死关头，一位妇人摔断了腿，她哀求别人给她一件救生衣。"但是没人这么做。

期间还是涌现出了一些英雄事迹。有些掉进海里的人没有救生衣，一群瑞典人就组成接力队伍，把救生衣扔给他们。一名男子跳进水里，游近一个救生筏并爬了上去。经过奋力拼搏，把很多人拉上了救生筏。但令人悲哀的是，不是每个人都能被救上来。这名男子后来回忆道："有个爱沙尼亚姑娘，我想抓住她，但是我的手指已经僵住了。一个大浪打到救生筏

---

wail *v.* 痛哭；悲叹　　　　　　　heroism *n.* 英雄主义；英雄事迹

◆ TRAGEDY IN THE BALTIC SEA

fingers were so *stiff*. She went down into the water when a big wave came over the [raft]."

Many passengers remained trapped deep inside the ship. Some of them woke up too late to get out. Others left their cabins in time but couldn't reach the upper deck. That was especially true for women, children, and older people. One investigator later explained why. "Getting up from the lower decks was very difficult," he said. "Passengers were faced with stairs that were upside down. The only way of climbing them would have been to hang monkey like from the railings. That requires strength."

Some of those who did get off the ship died anyway. The water was *frigid*. Once in the sea, many people *perished* from shock and exposure. Only those lucky enough to reach a life raft had any real chance. That was how one man survived. "I grabbed a life

---

上，她就沉到水里了。"

很多乘客仍旧被困在船舱深处。有的人醒得太晚，没跑出去。另外有些人，虽然及时离开了船舱，但没有办法爬到上层甲板去。尤其对妇女，儿童和老人，更是这样。一位调查人员后来解释了原因。他说："从下层甲板往上爬是很困难的。乘客们眼前是颠上倒下的楼梯。爬到上面的唯一方法就是抓紧扶手，像猴子一样吊在那里，这需要有力气。"

逃离了轮船的人中也有遇难的。海水非常寒冷。很多人休克而死或者被冻死。只有那些足够幸运，能爬上救生筏的人才有一丝活下来的希望。一名男子就是这样得以生还的。"我抓过一件救生衣，然后船的左舷就完

---

stiff *adj.* 僵直的；僵硬的  
perish *v.* 死亡

frigid *adj.* 寒冷的；严寒的

**TOTAL PANIC**

jacket," he said, "and then the [ferry] fell on its left side completely. I managed to jump into a rubber boat with three other people."

The first rescue ship arrived at 3:35 A.M. It was the Finnish ferry Mariella. Its captain was Jan Thure Törnroos. The night was dark, but Törnroos could see with the help of searchlights. It was a *grim* sight. "We could see people floating about in the water and hear them screaming for help," he said. "There were hundreds of bodies bobbing up and down."

Rescuing those who were still alive was not easy. The sea was very rough. Helicopters had to pull most of the people out of the water. The rescue effort went on for seven hours. Some people died waiting. Paul Barney made it to a *raft* with 11 other people. But icy waves kept breaking over their raft. Six of them died from the cold. "Every time we got slightly warmer," Barney said, "we got *drenched*

---

全沉下去了。我使劲跳上了一艘橡皮艇，那上面还有3个人。"

第一艘救生船于深夜3:35分抵达现场，是芬兰渡轮玛丽拉号，船长是简·瑟·汤鲁斯。夜里漆黑一片，但是借助于探照灯，汤鲁斯可以看见眼前的东西。真是非常可怕的一个场景。他说："我们能看到许多人漂在水里，并能听到他们的呼救声。几百个人在水里浮浮沉沉。"

营救那些还活着的人并不容易。海面波涛澎湃。直升机只能把大多数人拉出水面。营救工作持续了7个小时。在等待救援的时候，有些人就遇难了。保罗·巴尼爬上一个救生筏，上面还有11个人。但冰冷的海浪不断从筏上掠过。筏上有6个人被冻死。巴尼说："每次我们刚暖和一点，我

---

grim *adj.* 阴森的；令人生畏的　　　　　　　　raft *n.* 筏；救生筏
drench *v.* 使浸湿

◆ TRAGEDY IN THE BALTIC SEA

again."

In all, 859 people died. Of those, 765 went down with the ship. The Estonia became their tomb. Another 94 died after jumping from the *ferry*. In the end, just 137 people survived. Of those, only 26 were women and only 23 were younger than 18. The loss of the Estonia was one of the worst ferry disasters of all time. Prime Minister Carl Bildt of Sweden summed up everyone's feelings. It was, he said "a human *tragedy* beyond belief." And so it was.

---

们又全都湿透了。"

这次事故中共有859人死亡,其中有765人随着这艘船沉入大海。爱沙尼亚号成了他们的坟墓,另有94人在跳下渡轮后死亡。最后,有137人生还,其中妇女只有26人,年龄低于18岁的只有23人。爱沙尼亚号的失事是历史上发生在渡轮上的最严重的灾难之一。瑞典首相卡尔·彼得特概括了每个人的感受,他说,那是"难以置信的人间悲剧"。事实的确如此。

---

ferry  *n.*  渡船;摆渡                                tragedy  *n.*  悲剧

## TOTAL PANIC

## 12

# A Horrible Way to Die

Thirty-six-year-old Kimfumu had a *fever*. His head ached. And he had *diarrhea*. So in early April of 1995, Kimfumu went to the main hospital in Kikwit, Zaire (present-day Democratic Republic of the Congo). Doctors thought he had an infection in his intestines. They

*This is no ordinary funeral. The pallbearers are medical personnel protected by masks, gowns, and gloves against an invisible killer. That killer is the dreaded Ebola virus. Who will be its next victim?*

## 恐怖死亡路

这不是一次普通的葬礼。灵柩的护送者都是医务人员，他们带着面罩，穿着长袍，戴着手套，以此来保护自身免受一个隐形杀手的攻击。这个杀手就是致命的埃博拉病毒。谁将成为下一位受害者呢？

36岁的金夫姆发烧了，头也很痛，还伴有腹泻。1995年4月初，他住进了扎伊尔（现在的刚果民主共和国）基奎特一家重点医院。医生认为他得的是肠道传染病，所以就按照这种病症对他进行治疗，但是两天之后他的病情

---

fever  *n.*  发烧                                  diarrhea  *n.*  腹泻

◆ A HORRIBLE WAY TO DIE

treated him for it, but over the next two days he grew worse. At last, doctors chose to operate. They hoped to fix whatever was wrong inside Kimfumu's *belly*.

The operation turned into a nightmare. When doctors opened Kimfumu up, they found his insides were *dissolving*. His organs were literally turning to *mush*. There was nothing doctors could do to help him. They *sewed* him back up and tried to ease his pain. A nun named Sister Floralba took over his care. She knew about his condition. In fact, she had been present during the operation. As Sister Floralba watched in horror, blood began to pour from Kimfumu's nose. His ears and even his eyes began to bleed. On April 14, Kimfumu died.

By then, Sister Floralba herself was feeling ill. She, too, developed

---

加重了，最后，医生决定动手术。他们希望治好金夫姆肚子里的毛病。

这次手术最终变成了一场超级噩梦。医生们把金夫姆腹腔打开后，发现里面已经完全溃烂了，他的内脏器官已经逐渐变成糊状。没有哪个医生能挽救他的生命。医生们把金夫姆的腹腔缝合，并试图减轻他的痛苦程度。一位名叫希斯特·弗洛若巴的修女负责照顾他。希斯特知道金夫姆的情况。实际上，动手术时她也在场。她胆战心惊地看护着金夫姆，这时开始有血从金夫姆的鼻孔涌出。他的耳朵甚至眼睛也开始流血。4月14日，金夫姆死了。

那时，希斯特·弗洛若巴觉得自己也病了。她也开始发烧、头痛、腹泻。

---

belly *n.* 腹部
mush *n.* 糊状物

dissolve *v.* 溶解
sew *v.* 缝

**TOTAL PANIC**

a fever. She, too, had a headache and diarrhea. Three of her friends, all of them nuns, did what they could. They drove Sister Floralba 50 miles to a bigger hospital. But within days, she died the same horrifying death as Kimfumu had.

The next day, Sister Floralba's three friends became sick. One by one, they all died. By then, doctors realized what was happening. Some terrible disease was spreading through Kikwit. Each day, new cases came in. Victims all showed the same *hideous symptoms*. A few survived. But most were dying.

Doctors took blood samples from some of the victims. They rushed the samples to the United States. Doctors at the Centers for Disease Control (CDC) in Atlanta, Georgia, studied the samples. On May 11, CDC doctors announced their *findings*. They had figured

---

她的三个朋友，都是修女，尽了她们最大的努力，才把她送到50英里外一家更大的医院。但是几天之后，她和金夫姆一样，令人毛骨悚然地死去了。

第二天，希斯特·弗洛若巴那三个朋友也生病了，她们接连死去。此时，医生才意识到发生了什么。有一种可怕的疾病已经开始在基奎特传播。每天都有新的病例，被感染者都表现出相同的不堪入目的症状，只有几个人幸存下来，大部分都濒临死亡。

医生从部分被感染者身上采集了血样，并将其火速送往美国。坐落在佐治亚州亚特兰大的疾病控制中心里的医生们研究了这些样品。5月11日，疾病控制中心的医生公布了他们的发现。他们指出造成奎基特大量人

---

hideous *adj.* 可怕的；骇人听闻的     symptom *n.* 症状
finding *n.* 发现；调查结果

◆ A HORRIBLE WAY TO DIE

out what was causing the deaths in Kikwit. It was the dreaded Ebola virus.

Ebola was first identified in 1976. At that time, it killed about 400 people in another part of Zaire. Doctors knew the virus was deadly. They knew it spread through *contact* with a victim's blood. But they didn't know how the virus got into human blood in the first place. Dr. Peter Piot was one of the doctors who discovered Ebola. As he said in 1995, "Where Ebola comes from is a very big question mark."

Many doctors, including Dr. Piot, think Ebola comes from deep within Africa's rain *forests*. It may live in the body of some *rodent* or insect there. The virus probably does not harm this "host" creature. *As long as* the host has no contact with human beings, everything is fine. But now people are cutting down rain forests. So hosts and

死亡的元凶，就是致命的埃博拉病毒。

埃博拉病毒于1976年被首次识别出来。那次的埃博拉病毒导致了扎伊尔另一地区大约四百人死亡。医生们知道这种病毒是致命的，通过与患者血液的接触而传播。但是他们不知道最初这种病毒是如何进入人体血液中的。彼得·皮奥特是发现埃博拉病毒的医生中的一位，正如他1995年所说，"埃博拉病毒来自何方是一个巨大的疑问。"

很多医生，包括彼得·皮奥特，认为埃博拉病毒来自非洲热带雨林深处。埃博拉病毒可能存活在那里的某些啮齿动物和昆虫体内。这种病毒可能对其"寄主"生物来说是无害的，只要"寄主"生物不与人类接触，那就万事大吉了。但是如今人们正在砍伐热带雨林，这些"寄主"与人类

contact *n.* 接触
rodent *n.* 啮齿动物

forest *n.* 森林
as long as 只要

**TOTAL PANIC**

humans are meeting. As they do, the virus has a chance to enter the human body. And while the virus does not hurt the host, it is deadly to humans.

After the 1976 *outbreak*, the virus faded back into the rain forest. But then, in 1995, it had returned. By the time Sister Floralba's three friends died, terror filled the streets of Kikwit. Few people knew exactly what was happening. But they saw that death was all around them. By mid-May, 77 people had died. Each day, that number climbed higher.

Doctors from around the world rushed to Kikwit to help. A *horrendous* mess awaited them. The hospital where Kimfumu died was *filthy*. "People were *vomiting*," said one U.S. doctor. "There was... blood all over the floors and walls. The dead were lying among the

---

发生接触，因此这种病毒就有了进入人体的机会。虽然这种病毒不会对其"寄主"造成伤害，但于是对人类来说，它就是致命的。

1976年的那次爆发之后，这种病毒消失在热带雨林里。不过，在1995年，它卷土重来。希斯特·弗洛若巴的三位朋友死后，恐怖情绪就笼罩在基奎特的大街小巷。很少有人真正明白正在发生的事情，但是他们看到死亡就在周围不断上演。到5月中旬，已有77人死亡。每一天，死亡人数都在不断增加。

世界各地的医生都赶到基奎特来提供援助，可怕的混乱场面等待着他们。金夫姆死亡的那家医院里已经污秽不堪。一位美国医生说："病人不断地呕吐，那真是……地板上，墙壁上，到处都是血。人群里躺着许多死

---

outbreak  n.  爆发；暴动  
filthy  adj.  污秽的  

horrendous  adj.  可怕的  
vomit  v.  呕吐；吐出

◆ A HORRIBLE WAY TO DIE

living." There were no masks, no gowns, no clean *instruments*. Given the conditions, it was easy to see how virus-filled blood had spread from one person to the next.

There was another problem as well. By the time outside doctors arrived, many patients and staff members had fled in fear. That raised a *chilling* question. Were these runaways spreading the disease to other places? Would Ebola soon break out in bigger cities? Would it become a worldwide *plague*?

For days, people everywhere held their breath. It could take the virus up to 21 days to produce symptoms in a victim. So no one knew just how far it had spread. The government of Zaire closed all the schools in Kikwit. Medical clinics were also closed. Officials ordered people to stay in their homes. Still, every day, more and

---

人。"这里没有面罩，没有手套，也没有清洁设备。在这样的条件下，很容易看到携满病毒的血液从一个人身上扩散到相邻的人身上。

另外，还存在一个问题。当外来的医生到达此地的时候，很多病人和医护人员都产生了恐惧感逃走了。这引发了一个令人胆寒的问题：那些逃走的病人会不会把这种疾病传播到其他地方？埃博拉病毒是否很快就会在更大的城市中流行？它是否会演变成一场世界范围内的瘟疫？

一连数天，世界各地的人们都屏住了呼吸。因为直到感染的第二十一天，病毒才会在患者身上引发相关症状，所以没有人知道它的传播速度究竟有多快。扎伊尔政府封锁了基奎特的所有学校和医疗机构，政府官员告

---

instrument *n.* 设备  
plague *n.* 瘟疫

chilling *adj.* 使人恐惧的

**TOTAL PANIC**

more cases were reported.

Meanwhile, medical teams *fanned out* to nearby villages. They tried to explain the danger to people there. They begged villagers to treat their sick carefully. They *pleaded* with families to *refrain* from normal burial customs. Those customs involved handling the bloody organs of the dead person. If family members insisted on a normal burial, doctors urged them to wear rubber gloves.

Some people tried to do what the medical teams said. Others simply threw up their hands. "It's useless for us to do anything," said one villager. "What can we do against this disease?" Still others heard the news too late. A man named Mola had just finished burying his father when a medical team found him. "I don't know what to say," said Mola. "I am the one who helped [my father]. I

---

诫人们停留在家中。但是，每天还是有更多的病例被呈报上来。

此时，医疗队已经分散前往邻近的村庄。他们试图向那里的人们解释情况的危险性，请求村民们认真对待这种疾病。他们恳请家属改掉以往的丧葬习俗，这些习俗中包括触摸死者血淋淋的内脏器官，如果家庭成员坚持以往的丧葬方式，医生就要求他们戴上橡胶手套。

有些人尝试按照医疗队的告诫行事，有些人则放弃了努力。一位村民说："我们干什么都没有用。我们能为对抗这种疾病做什么呢？"还有一些人听到消息的时候已经太迟了。一位名叫莫拉的男子，在医疗队发现他的时候，刚刚埋葬了他的父亲。莫拉说："我真不知道说什么才好。我是给父亲送葬

---

fan out （使）展开；散开　　　　　　　　　plead v. 恳求
refrain v. 节制；戒除

have already touched the body. And now you tell me I must avoid contact?"

By May 26, 121 people had died of Ebola. Three weeks later, the number was up to 220. By July, it had gone to 315. But then—luckily—the virus died out. All the people who had been exposed to Ebola had either died or fought it off. By August 24, the *epidemic* was over.

Officials believe the Ebola virus still *lurks* in Africa's rain forests. It is there, hiding, in some host creature. We don't know what that host is. And we don't know when, if ever, Ebola will try to *leap* back into human bodies. But the threat of Ebola is a real one. It is one more reason why we should think twice before cutting down the world's remaining rain forests.

---

的人之一，我已经摸过他的尸体了。现在你告诉我别摸又有什么用呢？"

到了5月26日，已经有121人死于埃博拉病毒。3个星期后，死亡数字上升至220人。到了7月，死亡数字又上升至315人。此时——幸运的是——这种病毒销声匿迹了。感染上埃博拉病毒的人们，有些死掉了，另外一些最终将它击溃。到8月24日，疫情终于结束了。

官方相信，埃博拉病毒仍然潜伏在非洲的热带雨林里。在那里，这种病毒隐藏在一些"寄主"生物体内。我们并不知道"寄主"究竟是什么，也不知道，是否有可能，什么时候埃博拉病毒又会回到人类的身体中。但是埃博拉病毒的威胁的确是存在的。这是人类在砍伐世界上剩余的热带雨林时需要进行再三思考的另外一个原因。

---

epidemic *n.* 流行病；时疫　　　　　　　　　　　lurk *v.* 潜伏；埋伏
leap *v.* 跳；跳跃

TOTAL PANIC

# 13

# A Strangler Among Us

No one paid much attention to the first *murder*. After all, Boston had about 50 killings every year. The death of 55-year-old Anna Slesers looked like another *isolated* tragedy. She was found, strangled, in her home on June 14, 1962. Police figured a robber had killed her.

*If the man in this photo came to your apartment door in plumbers' overalls, would you let him in? Such costumes got Albert DeSalvo into the homes of several of his victims. DeSalvo, known as the Boston Strangler, murdered 13 women before his arrest in 1964.*

## 身边的谋杀犯

如果照片中的那位男子穿着水管工制服来到你的住宅门前,你会让他进去吗?一身这样的服装让阿尔伯特·德萨瓦进入了他的几名被害人家中。德萨瓦,众所周知的波士顿杀手,在1964年被捕之前,谋杀了13名妇女。

没有人对第一起谋杀案给予更多的关注。毕竟,波士顿每年都会有大约五十人被杀。55岁的安娜·斯莱瑟的死亡看上去只是又一起孤立的惨案。1962年6月14日,有人发现她在家中被勒死。警方认为是一个强盗杀害了她。

---

murder *n.* 谋杀                    isolated *adj.* 孤立的

◆ A STRANGLER AMONG US

Less than three weeks later, though, two more women were found dead in their homes. They, too, had been *strangled*. The crimes fit the same pattern as the Slesers case. When the police commissioner heard that, he felt sick. He knew he was not dealing with isolated killings. "Oh, God," he said. "We've got a madman loose."

And so began the panic that was to *grip* Boston for the next 18 months. Everyone began talking about the "Boston Strangler." The *commissioner* put extra detectives on the case. He canceled all police vacations. He set up a special emergency number that people could call anytime, day or night.

Beyond that, police urged women to keep their doors locked. They told people not to let strangers into their homes. The police also asked citizens to report any *suspicious* activity they saw.

---

　　但是，在接下来不到三个星期的时间内，又有两名妇女被发现死于家中。她们也是被勒死的，犯罪手段与斯莱瑟案中的手法相同。当警察局长听到这个消息的时候，他就好像是生病了一样。他知道正在办理的这些命案并不是彼此孤立的。他说："天哪！我们让一个疯子跑了出来。"

　　从那时起的18个月中，恐慌情绪笼罩着波士顿。每个人都在谈论着这个"波士顿杀手"。局长开始深入调查这个案件，他取消了警察局的所有假期，开通了一条专用应急热线，不论白天黑夜，人们在任何时候都可以拨打这个电话。

　　除此之外，警方要求妇女们锁好房门，告诫妇女不要让陌生人进入家中。警方还要求市民报告看到的任何可疑迹象。

---

strangle　*v.* 把……勒死　　　　　　　　　　grip　*v.* 掌握；控制
commissioner　*n.* 警察局长　　　　　　　　suspicious　*adj.* 可疑的

**TOTAL PANIC**

But it did no good. In August, the killer struck again. Two more women were strangled. They were 75-year-old Ida Irga and 67-year-old Jane Sullivan. Both were found dead in their apartments. Police were sure it was the work of the strangler. For one thing, there was no sign of forced entry. Both Irga and Sullivan—like the others—had let the killer in without a fight. As in the other cases, the apartments had been *ransacked*, but nothing had been taken. Finally, the murderer had left his "signature": a bow, tied and *knotted* in a special way around the victims' necks.

Now the people of Boston were really *petrified*. Women refused to open their doors to delivery men. They screamed when salesmen rang their doorbells. Local hardware stores sold out of *security* locks. The Animal Rescue League couldn't keep up with the demand for

---

但是情况并没有好转。八月份，杀手再次作案。又有两名妇女被勒死，她们是75岁的艾达·伊格和67岁的简·沙利文。两个人都是被发现死在自家住宅中。警方相信这一定是那个杀手所为。首先，现场没有杀手强行闯入住宅的迹象。伊格和沙利文——与其他被害人一样——并没有经过搏斗，就让杀手进入家中。与其他案件一样，住宅里被彻底搜查过，但是并没有东西被拿走。最后，谋杀犯留下了他的"标志"：在被害人的脖子四周，有一个通过特殊方式系好的蝴蝶结。

现在波士顿人真的是惊呆了。妇女不再给邮差开门，推销员按门铃时，她们就会高声尖叫。当地五金商店里的保险锁销售一空，动物救助协

---

ransack v. 彻底搜索；仔细搜查　　　　　knot v. 打结
petrify v. 使……惊呆　　　　　　　　　security n. 安全

◆ A STRANGLER AMONG US

watchdogs. Every day, women in tears called the police to report strange-looking men near their buildings.

One woman, who was expecting a visit from a friend, heard a knock on her door. She opened it. But instead of her friend, she was met by a man she had never seen before. Was it the Boston Strangler? Actually, it was someone selling *encyclopedias*. But the woman didn't know that. She was so terrified that she had a heart attack and dropped dead *on the spot*.

As panic swept through the city, the police struggled to find the killer. They looked at every possible clue. All the victims were white women over the age of 50. Did the killer meet them at some event for the elderly? All the dead women were also big music lovers. Did the strangler find them at concerts or music stores? Or perhaps the

---

会里的看门犬供不应求。每天都有泪流满面的妇女向警察报告房屋周围出现了陌生男子。

一位妇人正在家中打算招待一个朋友，这时她听到有人敲门。但是她看到的不是她的朋友，而是一个从未见过面的男子。他是波士顿杀手吗？实际上，这只是一个来送百科全书的人，但这位妇人不清楚。她非常惊恐，结果突发心脏病，倒在地上死了。

恐慌情绪席卷了整个城市。警方尽全力捉拿杀手，不放过每一条可能的线索。所有的被害人都是50岁以上的白人妇女。杀手曾经在某些为老年人举办的活动当中见过她们吗？所有的死者都是狂热的音乐爱好者，凶犯是在音乐会或者音乐专卖店里见到过她们的吗？也许答案应该从另一个角

---

encyclopedia  *n.*  百科全书　　　　　　　　　　　　　on the spot  当场

**TOTAL PANIC**

answer lay in a different direction. All the victims were somehow connected to hospitals. They either worked at one or had just been treated at one. Was the killer also connected to hospitals in some way?

These possibilities led nowhere. And in the meantime, the killings continued. By the end of the year, the strangler had claimed two more victims. These two, however, were different. Both women were young—in their early twenties. In addition, one was black. The strangler was *varying* his crimes. With his next victim, he added another twist. This woman was found *stabbed* as well as strangled. Nonetheless, many details of the crime were the same. The murders all seemed to have been carried out by one man.

Police were *frustrated*. Everyone had been warned about the

---

度来寻找。所有被害人都与医院有着某些联系。她们或者是在某家医院工作，或者刚刚去医院看过病。杀手会与医院有着某种联系吗？

这些可能性还是让人理不出头绪。与此同时，凶杀案继续发生着。到这年年末，这个谋杀犯又杀了两个人。但是这两个人与以往的有所不同。两名妇女都很年轻——都是刚刚20出头。另外，其中有一位黑人。凶手改变了作案手段。在下一位被害人身上，这个杀手又加了一点花样，这名妇女除了被勒死之外，身上还有被刺伤的痕迹。然而，很多作案细节都是相同的。这些谋杀案看上去是同一名男子实施的。

警方感到非常沮丧。他们已经向每个人警告过波士顿杀手的情况，但

---

vary  v. 改变；使多样化　　　　　　　　　　　　　　　　　　stab  v. 刺伤
frustrate  v. 挫败；使感到灰心

◆ A STRANGLER AMONG US

Boston Strangler, yet again and again he was able to talk his way into his victims' apartments. How was he doing it? And why?

One clue came from a woman named Gertrude Gruen. She lived through an attack by the Boston Strangler. In February of 1963, someone knocked on her apartment door. It was a man dressed in workman's clothing. He told her he had come to fix a leak in her *bathroom*. There were other workmen in the area, so she *assumed* he was part of the same crew. She let him in. But when she turned her back on him, he threw his arm around her neck and tried to strangle her.

Gruen kicked and *thrashed*, trying to get away. She managed to grab her attacker's finger between her teeth. Then she *bit* down hard, almost to the bone. He loosened his hold on her for a minute

杀手还是屡次进入被害人的住宅。他是怎么做的？他又为什么这么做呢？

有一条线索来自一位名叫格楚德·格鲁恩的妇人。她在波士顿杀手的袭击中幸存下来。1963年2月，有人来敲她的房门。这是一名穿着工人服装的男子，他告诉这位妇人，他是来修理她家浴室漏水的。这一地区还有其他工人，所以这位妇人以为他只是其中的一个并让他进了屋，但当她转过身去的时候，这名男子用胳膊缠住她的脖子，试图勒死她。

格鲁恩拳打脚踢，试图逃跑。她想方设法地用牙齿咬住攻击者的手指，然后用力咬了下去，几乎要咬到骨头了。过了一会儿，这名男子把她放开

---

bathroom *n.* 浴室
thrash *v.* 打；痛击

assume *v.* 假定
bite *v.* 咬

## TOTAL PANIC

and she screamed. Through the window, she could see workmen on the roof turn and look in her direction. The strangler must have seen them too. He *released* her and fled from the apartment.

Gruen's story didn't explain why the strangler killed women. But it did help explain how he got into their apartments. After that, real repairmen found it harder and harder to get their work done. Many women simply would not let them in. And some women didn't stop there. They began *toting* tear gas bombs in their purses. Some carried long hatpins with them wherever they went. They hoped to fend off any attack with one sharp jab of the pin. Some women even took up karate.

Nothing, however, seemed to stop the strangler. By January of 1964, the death toll stood at 13. The victims were all women, but

---

了，她尖叫起来。通过窗户，她看见房顶有几个工人转身向她这边看了过来。这个谋杀犯肯定也看见他们了，这名男子丢开她，从住宅逃走了。

格鲁恩的经历并没有揭示出这名谋杀犯杀害妇女的原因，但足够有利于说明杀手进入住宅的方式。从那之后，真正的修理工发现进行工作越来越难了。很多妇女干脆不让他们进门。不仅如此，她们还在手提包里装上催泪弹。有些妇女不论走到哪里都随身带着长长的帽针，希望能用帽针锐利的尖端抵挡住可能的突然袭击。有些妇女甚至开始学习空手道。

但是，似乎没有什么力量可以阻止谋杀犯的行动。截至1964年1月，死亡人数达到13人。被害人全是妇女，但除此之外，没有发现任何犯罪特征。被

---

release *v.* 放松；松开　　　　　　　　　　　　　　tote *v.* 携带

◆ A STRANGLER AMONG US

beyond that, no clear pattern emerged. The victims ranged in age from 19 to 85. Some had been killed on weekends, some during the week. Most lived alone, but a couple had *roommates*. Most were white, but one was black. Most had been strangled with a pair of stockings, but one had been stabbed and one had been beaten to death with a brass pipe.

Police followed up on every lead they got, no matter how unlikely it seemed. They fed all the information they had into computers, hoping to find a link to some known *criminal*. They even turned to *psychics* for help.

In the end, though, it was the strangler himself who solved the case. In the fall of 1964, a man was arrested for breaking into a home. The *intruder* was 33-year-old Albert DeSalvo. He had been in

---

害人的年龄在19岁至85岁之间。有些人是在周末被杀害的,有些人是在一周的其他时间被杀害的。大多数被害人都是独居的,但也有一些是与他人合住的;大多数被害人是白人,但是有一名被害者是黑人;大多数被害人是被长筒袜勒死的,但是有一人身上有刺伤痕迹,有一人被用铜管殴打致死。

　　警方追踪了所得的每一条线索,不管那条线索看上去有多么不可思议。他们把得到的所有信息输入电脑,希望能从已知的犯罪行为中找到联系。他们甚至向巫师寻求帮助。

　　但是,最后还是谋杀犯自己了结了这个案件。1964年秋天,一名男子因闯入民宅而被捕。这名入侵者就是33岁的阿尔伯特·德萨瓦,他以前

---

roommate  *n.*  室友
psychic  *n.*  巫师

criminal  *n.*  罪犯
intruder  *n.*  入侵者

**TOTAL PANIC**

trouble before. In fact, he had just been released from prison in April 1962. That was two months before the strangler first struck. Police had no idea that DeSalvo was connected to the killings. But he gave himself away. He bragged to a *cellmate*, saying he was the Boston Strangler.

When police heard this, they questioned DeSalvo about it. Yes, he said, he had *committed* the murders. He could not explain what had *prompted* him to kill. And he could not explain why he had chosen those particular women. Yet he knew dozens of details that only the killer could have known. And so in the end, there could be no doubt. DeSalvo was the Boston Strangler. When the people of Boston learned that the madman had been caught, they all breathed a sigh of *relief*. Now, after months of terror, the city could finally return to normal.

---

就进过监狱。实际上，1962年4月，在谋杀犯首次作案前的两个月，他刚刚被释放出来。警察根本没把德萨瓦和这些谋杀案联系起来，但是他自己招认了。他向一个同伙吹嘘说，他是波士顿杀手。

听完这些诉说，警察开始审问德萨瓦。是的，如他所说，他对这些谋杀行为供认不讳。他没有解释自己的杀人动机，也没有解释为什么选择那些特定的妇女作为作案对象，但是他知道很多只有杀手自己才有可能知道的细节。最后，毫无疑问，德萨瓦就是波士顿杀手。当波士顿人得知那个疯子已经被抓住时，他们都长出了一口气。现在，在经历了几个月的恐慌之后，这座城市终于恢复了正常。

---

cellmate *n.* 同牢房的人  
prompt *v.* 促使；导致  
commit *v.* 犯罪；做错事  
relief *n.* 宽慰；解脱

# 14

# The Richard Riot

Canadians knew there might be trouble. Still, on the night of March 17, 1955, ice *hockey* fans turned out in force. They packed the Forum in the Quebec city of Montreal. They were not in a happy mood. To make things worse, the most-hated man in Quebec had *announced* that he

*Angry fans attack Clarence Campbell, the president of the National Hockey League, during a game at the Forum in Montreal, Canada. The violence quickly spread to the city's streets.*

## 理查德骚乱

在加拿大蒙特利尔体育场举行的一场比赛期间，愤怒的球迷袭击了国家冰球协会主席克莱伦斯·坎贝尔。暴力行动很快蔓延到这座城市的大街小巷。

加拿大人知道可能会有麻烦了。1955年3月17日夜间，冰球迷们将这种可能变成了现实。他们聚集在魁北克省蒙特利尔市的体育场里。他们的情绪非常糟糕。但更糟糕的是，魁北克最令人痛恨的人宣布他会亲临这次比

---

hockey *n.* 冰球　　　　　　　　　　　announce *v.* 宣布

## TOTAL PANIC

would be at the game. It seemed only a matter of time. Sooner or later, a *riot* was sure to break out.

That most-hated man was Clarence Campbell, president of the National Hockey League. He had just *suspended* Maurice "The Rocket" Richard (Ree shard) for the rest of the year. A week earlier, Richard had twice swung his hockey stick at another player. Such violent acts sometimes happen in hockey. Most of the time the players involved get a fine or a short suspension. But this time Campbell had cracked down really hard.

If it had happened to a *lesser* player, the fans' anger might just have blown over. But Richard was a superstar. He was the best player on the Montreal Canadiens. Without him, the team had little chance of winning the Stanley Cup.

---

赛现场。看上去只是时间问题，迟早会发生一场骚乱。

那个最令人痛恨的人就是克莱伦斯·坎贝尔，国家冰球协会主席。他刚刚宣布莫里斯"火箭"理查德本年度的剩余时间内不能参加比赛。一星期前，理查德向另外一名运动员两次挥动曲棍。类似的暴力行为在冰球运动中时常发生。大多数情况下，卷入其中的运动员都会被处以罚金或者被短期停赛。但是这一次，坎贝尔实施的处罚太严重了。

如果这种情况发生在一个非主力球员身上，球迷们的愤怒情绪就有可能慢慢缓和。但是理查德是一名超级巨星，他是蒙特利尔加拿大队中最出色的球员。如果没有他，这支球队就几乎没有机会赢得斯坦利杯了。

---

riot *n.* 暴乱；骚乱  
lesser *adj.* 次要的

suspend *v.* 中止；暂停

◆ THE RICHARD RIOT

And there was more. Richard was a *symbol* of great pride for the people of Quebec. Like most people from Quebec, Richard spoke French. That set him apart from people in other parts of Canada. Campbell was from an English-speaking part of Canada. So to some fans, it seemed as if Campbell was punishing not just a player or a team but every French speaker in Quebec.

Newspapers and radio stations stirred up hatred for Campbell. A cartoon showed Campbell's head on a *platter*. The *caption* read: "This is how we would like to see him." One poll showed that 97 percent of the Quebec people surveyed felt the punishment was too *harsh*. Brian McKenna, who later made a film about Richard, was nine years old at the time. He said, "It was my first sense that maybe the world was unfair." Even the mayor of Montreal criticized Campbell's

---

　　他被停赛这件事情还有更严重的影响。理查德是魁北克人强烈自豪感中一个象征性的符号。与大多数来自魁北克的人一样，理查德说的是法语。这一点将他与加拿大其他地区的人区别开来。坎贝尔来自加拿大说英语的地区。所以对一些球迷来说，似乎坎贝尔惩罚的不仅仅是一名运动员或一支球队，而是魁北克省说法语的每个人。

　　报纸和广播电台不断煽动对坎贝尔的仇视情绪。在一部卡通片里，坎贝尔的脑袋出现在一个托盘上，字幕这样写道："这就是我们对待坎贝尔的态度。"一项民意测验显示，被调查的魁北克人中有97%觉得这项处罚太苛刻了。布赖恩·麦肯纳，一位日后制作了一部关于理查德的电影的人，当时只有9岁。他说："我的第一感觉是，可能这个世界太不公平了。"甚至蒙特利尔市市长都出面批评了坎贝尔的决定。

---

symbol *n.* 象征
caption *n.* 字幕；标题

platter *n.* 大平盘
harsh *adj.* 严厉的；严酷的

## TOTAL PANIC

decision.

To add more heat to the *simmering* pot, Campbell announced that he would be at the Forum on March 17. The mayor begged him to stay home. But Campbell wanted to go. He often went to games there. He didn't see any reason why he should back down. "I have a right to go," he said.

Campbell was not there when the game began. A few minutes into the first period, Richard arrived with his wife. No one even noticed him. All eyes were on Campbell's empty seat. Halfway through the first period, the Detroit Red Wings took a 2-0 lead. Any hopes of the Canadiens' winning seemed to be *evaporating*. At that moment Campbell walked into the Forum. He didn't try to *sneak* in or come in *disguise*. He wanted the fans to know he wasn't afraid.

---

火上浇油的是，坎贝尔宣布他会出现在3月17日的体育场内。市长请求他留在家中，但坎贝尔坚持要去。他经常去那里观看比赛，他觉得没有任何理由放弃，他说："我有去那儿的权力。"

比赛开始时坎贝尔还没有到达那里。第一节比赛进行了几分钟后，理查德携妻子到达现场，根本没有人注意他，所有人的眼睛都盯着坎贝尔那个空着的座位。第一节比赛进行到一半，底特律红翼队以2：0领先，加拿大队获胜的任何希望似乎都破灭了。正在这时，坎贝尔走进体育场，他既没有鬼鬼祟祟，也没有作任何伪装，就进去了。他想让球迷们知道他没有什么可害怕的。

---

simmer *v.* 煨；炖  
sneak *v.* 偷偷地走；溜  
evaporate *v.* 消失  
disguise *n.* 假扮；伪装

◆ **THE RICHARD RIOT**

The crowd roared with *disgust*. They began to shout "Shoo Campbell, Shoo Campbell." A few fans threw eggs, tomatoes, and programs at him. At one point, a flying object knocked the hat off his head. An orange hit Campbell in the back. "This is a *disgrace*," muttered Richard, who saw what was happening.

Campbell refused to *budge*. During the intermission after the first period, a fan walked up to Campbell's *aisle* seat. The man stuck out his hand as if to offer a handshake. Campbell put out his hand. But instead of shaking Campbell's hand, the fan slapped his face. Many outraged fans rushed to surround Campbell. Would they kill him?

We will never know. At that moment, someone in the crowd tossed a tear-gas bomb only 25 feet from Campbell. Everyone panicked. They forgot about Campbell. All they wanted was to get

---

人群之中发出愤怒的吼声。他们就开始大喊："嘘——坎贝尔！嘘——坎贝尔！"少数球迷开始向他扔鸡蛋、西红柿和赛程表，不知从哪里飞过来一个东西把他的帽子从头顶撞了下来，一个橘子击中坎贝尔的后背。看着发生的一切，理查德低语着："真是丢人！"

坎贝尔拒绝退场。在第一节比赛之后的中场休息时间里，一名球迷走向坎贝尔在过道边的座席，这名男子伸出一只手，好像是要和他握手，于是坎贝尔也伸出一只手，但是这名球迷没有和他握手，而是给了他一记耳光。许多愤怒的球迷冲过来包围了坎贝尔，他们是不是想要杀了他？

我们永远不会知道了。此刻，人群之中，有个人在距坎贝尔只有25英尺远的地方扔了一枚催泪弹，每个人都惊慌失措，他们忘掉了坎贝尔，都想尽

---

disgust  *n.*  厌恶
budge  *v.*  让步

disgrace  *n.*  丢脸；耻辱
aisle  *n.*  通道；侧廊

**TOTAL PANIC**

out of the Forum as fast as possible. "The bomb-thrower," said a police chief, "protected Campbell's life by releasing [the bomb] at precisely the right moment."

Campbell fled to the first-aid center. "This is terrible," he said. "People might have been killed." He then *called off* the rest of the game and *declared* it a forfeit in favor of the Red Wings.

By then, frightened fans had rushed out onto the street. Once there, some of them *vented* their rage. They began what would be called "The Richard Riot." It was started by only a few hundred troublemakers. But, as in any mob scene, others got swept up in the madness. In a short time, a mob of more than 10,000 people was shouting "Kill Campbell!" Gangs of mostly young fans broke windows, set fires, tipped over cars, and *looted* stores. This

---

快离开体育场。警察局长说："扔炸弹的人在恰当的时刻，恰当的地方扔了催泪弹，这真是救了坎贝尔一命。"

坎贝尔逃到急救中心。他说："太可怕了，这些人都该去死！"然后他取消了剩余的比赛，并且宣布以支持红翼队而告终。

这时，惊慌失措的球迷已经冲到大街上。在大街上，有些人开始发泄他们的愤怒情绪，他们开始上演了所谓的"理查德骚乱"。这是由这仅有的数百名捣乱分子引发的。但是，正如在任何一个大型集会中一样，在疯狂的人群中，这种骚动迅速传播开来。不久，一大群民众，总数超过10,000人，开始高喊："杀死坎贝尔！"一群球迷，其中大多数都是年轻人，开始砸玻璃，放

---

call off 取消　　　　　　　　　　　　declare *v.* 宣布；宣告
vent *v.* 发泄感情　　　　　　　　　loot *v.* 抢劫

◆ THE RICHARD RIOT

continued for four long hours. By the time the riot petered out, police had arrested 137 people.

Earlier, Richard had left the Forum by a back door. At home, he listened to riot reports on the radio. He couldn't believe what was being done in his name. He felt badly. "Once I felt like going downtown and telling the people over a loudspeaker to stop their *nonsense*," Richard said. "But it wouldn't have done any good. They would have carried me around on their shoulders." Richard thought it was nice to have fans support him, but he knew these fans were doing it the wrong way.

Fortunately, no one was killed. Still, many people in Montreal felt *remorse*. The next day one sportswriter wrote, "I am ashamed of my city."

---

火,掀翻汽车,抢劫商店。这种场面持续了4小时之久。截止暴乱平息时,警方共逮捕了137人。

事情发生不久,理查德已经从后门离开体育场。在家中,他收听广播,得知了骚乱的消息。他不敢相信这些以他的名义所做的事情。他感觉非常糟糕。理查德说:"我曾经想到现场去,用大喇叭告诉那些人停止这些愚蠢的行为,但这么做是没用的。他们会把我扛在肩膀上。"理查德认为有球迷支持他,这是很好的,但是他知道,这些球迷的做法已经走入歧途。

所幸没有人在事件中死亡。但是很多蒙特利尔人仍然感到非常愧疚。第二天,体育新闻记者写道:"我为我的城市感到耻辱。"

---

nonsense *n.* 胡闹;愚蠢的举动     remorse *n.* 痛恨;自责

TOTAL PANIC

Others, however, still blamed Campbell. They said he had *provoked* the riot by showing up. Some still *mumbled* about getting even. The threat of a second riot hung in the air. Hoping to *diffuse* the dangerous situation, Richard decided to speak up.

On March 18 he spoke in French to his fans. He said it was hard not being able to play, but there was nothing he could do about it. He urged his fans to stop all the violence. "So that no further harm will be done," he added, "I would like to ask everyone to get behind the team and to help the boys win... I will take my punishment and come back next year to help the club."

Richard's speech calmed the city. There was no more violence. But in the long run, the Richard Riot helped *spark* a new movement in Canada that is still alive today. It had nothing to do with hockey.

但是，仍旧有人谴责坎贝尔。他们说是他的出现引发了这场骚乱。一些人仍然在嘀咕着要讨回公道。骚乱再一次爆发的危险弥漫在空中。为了缓和这种危险的形势，理查德决定公开表态。

3月18日，理查德用法语向他的球迷发表讲话。他说返回球坛是很困难的，但是他对此无能为力。他劝说球迷们停止一切暴力活动。他补充道："所以别再做傻事了，我希望每个人都为球队站脚助威，帮助这些孩子取得胜利……我会接受处罚，明年再来为俱乐部效力。"

理查德的讲话使这座城市慢慢平静下来，暴力活动不再出现。但是最后，理查德骚乱引发了在加拿大持续至今的一项新的运动。这不是对冰球

provoke v. 引起；激起
diffuse v. 传播；扩散

mumble v. 含糊地说；咕哝着说
spark v. 引发

◆ THE RICHARD RIOT

It had to do with the French people of Quebec. They began a long fight to *preserve* their culture and language. Some even wanted to make Quebec a separate nation.

This movement has been called the Quiet *Revolution*. Sportswriter Red Fisher was covering his first game ever on the night of the Richard Riot. Fisher later wrote, "If that was the start of the Quiet Revolution, it wasn't very quiet."

---

运动而言的，而是对魁北克省法语人口而言的。他们开始了一项长期的为保护他们的文化和语言而进行的斗争。甚至有人想使魁北克成为一个独立国家。

这项运动被称为"魁北克革命"。体育新闻记者雷德·费希尔，在发生理查德骚乱的那一夜，正在完成它的首篇报道。费希尔后来写道："如果说那是魁北克革命的开端，那么这个开端是非常不平静的。"

---

preserve  *v.*  保护；维护

revolution  *n.*  革命

TOTAL PANIC

# 15

# A Volcano Wakes Up

Sure, El Chichón was a *volcano*. But it had not *erupted* in many, many years. In fact, most scientists said the volcano had been inactive for thousands of years. El Chichón was also quite small—it was really little more than a hill. It stood only 4,134 feet high. Even its name

*A column of volcanic smoke and ash from El Chichn rises 12,000 feet above the village of El Volcan. Residents of the town, like everyone else living in this area of southern Mexico, were driven away when the small mountain suddenly erupted on March 28, 1982.*

## 苏醒的火山

一柱火山烟灰从埃尔奇琼山头升起，高达12,000英尺，笼罩在埃维肯村上空。与其他居住在墨西哥南部这一地区的人们一样，1982年3月28日，当这座小火山突然爆发时，这个村庄的居民们都夺路而逃。

可以肯定，埃尔奇琼山确实是一座火山，但是它已经很多很多年没有爆发了。实际上，大多数科学家认为这座火山已经休眠了几千年了。埃尔奇琼火山也实在是太小了——实际上它比一座小山还要小，只有4134英尺高。甚至

volcano  n.  火山                              erupt  v.  爆发

### ◆ A VOLCANO WAKES UP

wasn't *scary*. In the local language, Chichón means "lump."

So there was no need to worry. Or was there? A volcano will often give some warning signs before it erupts. El Chichón, in southern Mexico, began sending out such signals in the early 1980s. For months the earth made *rumbling* sounds. There were even a few small earthquakes. A cloud of steam appeared over El Chichón. Also, the water in local rivers began heating up and giving off the odor of *sulfur*.

These were all hints that the volcano might erupt. But they offered no guarantee. Maybe nothing would happen. Officials said the earth in the region had always rumbled. They declared that the cloud of steam had always been there. So nothing was done. The Zoque Indians who lived near El Chichón were never instructed to

---

它的名字也不会让人害怕。在当地的语言里，埃尔奇琼的意思是"小东西"。

所以根本没有必要担心。又有什么可担心的呢？一座火山在爆发之前通常都会有一些预兆。墨西哥南部的这座埃尔奇琼火山，在19世纪80年代初开始发出这样一些征兆。连月来，地面都发出了阵阵轰隆声，甚至发生了几次小型地震。一团蒸汽云出现在埃尔奇琼火山山头。当地的河水也开始变热，并且散发出硫黄的气味。

这一切都暗示着火山可能要爆发。但是这些情况也并不能为火山爆发提供任何保证，也许什么都不会发生。官员们说这一区域内的地面经常会发出轰隆声。他们说那团蒸汽云总是停留在那里，所以人们不用作任何防备。从未有人通知居住在埃尔奇琼火山附近的索克印第安人搬走。事后证

---

scary *adj.* 恐怖的；吓人的  
sulfur *n.* 硫黄

rumbling *adj.* 隆隆声的

**TOTAL PANIC**

move out. That turned out to be a terrible mistake.

By March of 1982, the rumblings had grown stronger. At last, scientists decided to check things out. But they didn't act quickly enough. Late on the night of March 28, El Chichon blew its top. It *spewed* ash 10 miles into the darkening sky.

As the *ash* fell back to earth, it covered everything. "About a billion tons of ash fell over a 10-square-mile area," said one official. The volcano also shot out hot gases and rocks. "There's nothing left on the mountain," said one man, "only stones and ashes."

Those who lived nearby had little or no chance to get away. The volcano rained down fire and ash on local villages. It totally wiped out several communities. One of these was called Nicalpa. It was located just four miles from the volcano. "My five children burned to

---

明，这是一个非常可怕的错误。

　　到1982年3月，轰隆声变得更剧烈了。最后，科学家们决定彻底检查一下。但是他们的行动不够迅速。3月28日后半夜，埃尔奇琼火山突然爆发了，向黑暗的天空中喷涌出了足有10英里高的火山灰。

　　火山灰落到了地面，把所有东西都掩盖起来。一位官员说："在10平方英里范围内落下了大约十亿吨火山灰。"火山还喷发出灼热的气体和熔岩。一名男子说："山上什么都没留下，只有石块和灰烬。"

　　住在附近的居民只有很少，甚至没有逃生的机会。当地的村庄里到处都是火山爆发引燃的大火和喷发出来的火山灰。火山爆发摧毁了几个部落，其中之一叫作尼卡帕。这个部落就坐落在距火山4英里的地方。这里的一位居民说："我的5个孩子都被烧死了。我去找他们的时候，发现那

---

spew *v.* 喷出；放出　　　　　　　　　　　　　　　　　　ash *n.* 灰

◆ A VOLCANO WAKES UP

death," said one *resident*. "When I went to look for them, I found only ashes. The house wasn't there anymore."

Another man was away from Nicalpa at the time. But when he returned, he found his farm destroyed. "I had 20 cattle and a few horses," he said sadly. "The fire that came burned everything. I had corn, beans, and coffee, and everything now is flat ground." Some of his friends were not even that lucky. One family of seven was caught near the village. The entire family died.

The March 28 eruption was bad enough, but the worst was yet to come. A volcano is difficult to *predict*. Will it produce just one eruption or will there be others? If there is more than one, how big will the next ones be? Not even the experts could answer those questions. The people who lived just out of range of the first

---

里只剩下一片灰烬，房子也没了。"

当时，还有一名男子从尼卡帕里逃出来。但当返回那里的时候，他发现自己的农场已经被毁掉了。他难过地说："我原来有20头牛和几间房子，大火把所有东西都烧光了。我还有玉米、豆子、咖啡，现在全被埋在下面了。"他的几个朋友也非常不幸。有一个七口之家就在这个村庄附近，大火烧过之后，全家人都死了。

3月28日的火山爆发已经够糟糕的了，但是更糟糕的还在后面。火山活动难以预测，这座火山是只爆发一次，还是会再爆发几次呢？如果爆发不止一次，那么下一次的爆发会有多么剧烈呢？甚至是专家们也无法回答这个问题。原来居住在第一次爆发外围的人们不知道应该怎么办。他们是应

---

resident *n.* 居民　　　　　　　　　　　　　　predict *v.* 预言；预测

## TOTAL PANIC

explosion didn't know what to do. Should they stay in their homes? Should they leave? In the end, officials decided these people had to be *evacuated*. Many were forced out of their homes against their will. Some refused to stay away and quickly snuck back to their villages.

Tragically for them, on April 2, El Chichón acted up again. It began sending out more ash and gas. The noon sky turned black. Many people were really frightened, fearing the darkening sky was a sign from God. They believed that they were being punished for their *sins*. Most of these people felt certain that they were all about to die. A local *priest* spoke to them over the radio, trying to calm their fears. The priest explained that the darkness was caused by the ash in the air. It was just a natural *phenomenon*.

Most villagers listened to the priest. But the following day, El

---

该在家呢？还是应该离开呢？最后，官方决定人们必须撤离。迫于压力，很多人不情愿地离开家园。有些人拒绝离开，很快偷偷溜回自己的村庄。

他们的命运十分悲惨。4月2日，埃尔奇琼火山再次开始活动，喷发出更多的灰烬和气体，天空很快变成了黑色。很多人确实感到害怕了，担心黑暗的天空是上帝发出的警告。他们相信他们正在为自己的罪恶而接受惩罚。大多数人认为自己必死无疑。当地的一位牧师通过广播向他们发表讲话，试图平息他们心中的恐惧感。这位牧师解释说，黑暗是由弥漫在空中的火山灰引起的，这只是一种自然现象。

大多数村民听信了牧师的话。但是第二天，埃尔奇琼火山再次爆发。

---

evacuate v. 撤离　　　　　　　　　　　sin n. 过失；罪恶
priest n. 牧师　　　　　　　　　　　　phenomenon n. 现象

### ◆ A VOLCANO WAKES UP

Chichón erupted again. This was the worst explosion of all. Gas, ash, and rocks came pouring out of the volcano. One man said, "It looked like fireworks were blasting out of the [volcano's] top." The eruption continued into the next day. Thousands of people fled their homes. Some made it to safety; many didn't.

This time, the volcano reached as far as the town of Pichucalco, about 15 miles away. Ash and rocks caused *tremendous* damage there. The roof of the new market *collapsed*, as did the roof of the town's only movie theater. "The fire started coming out of the sky," said one man. "[The] rocks came through the roof like bullets." These "fire rocks," as they were called, burned and injured many people.

The blast *wiped out* the small village of Francisco León. It was located in a valley, so the flow of burning lava was funneled straight

---

这次爆发是所有爆发中最剧烈的一次。气体、灰烬和熔岩从火山口喷涌而出。一名男子说："看上去就像火焰从[火山]上面喷出来似的。"这次爆发一直持续到次日。几千人逃离家园，有些人安全了，但很多人没有。

这一次，火山爆发波及范围远至15英里外的皮楚卡格镇。火山灰和熔岩给那里造成了巨大的破坏。新建市场的房顶被掀掉，镇里唯一的电影院的顶棚也被摧毁了。一名男子说："大火腾空而起，岩块就像子弹一样扫过屋顶。"这些"火块"，他们这样称呼，烧死烧伤了很多人。

突如其来的打击摧毁了小村庄弗朗西斯科·利昂。这个村庄坐落在一个山谷中，所以熔岩流顺着山谷直冲进去。熔岩把村庄里肥沃的土壤变成

---

tremendous *adj.* 巨大的  
wipe out 消灭；彻底摧毁

collapse *v.* 倒塌；崩溃

## TOTAL PANIC

into it. The lava turned the village's *fertile* fields into a *barren* desert. It turned the trees into charcoal. And it turned people's dreams to dust.

Everyone who was caught in the village died. Rescue workers didn't reach the area until two weeks later. They found the whole place buried under ash. Only a small section of the church wall was still *visible*. The first body they dug up was that of a little boy. He was hugging his small dog.

El Chichón was a major eruption. After the blast, the top 700 feet of the mountain were gone. The blast sent a huge amount of ash into the air. This ash affected the world's weather. High in the atmosphere, the ash reflected sunlight away from the planet. That, in turn, lowered temperatures on Earth.

---

不毛之地，把树木变成焦炭，使人们的梦想彻底破灭。

　　这个村子里受灾的每一个人都死掉了。救援人员两周之后才抵达那里。他们发现整个地方都被烧成一片灰烬。只有一座教堂的一小部分还能够被辨认出来。他们挖出的第一具尸体是一个小男孩的，他正紧紧地抱着他的小狗。

　　埃尔奇琼火山正处在主爆发期。那次爆发后，山头被削低了700英尺。爆发把巨量火山灰喷到空中。这些火山灰影响了全世界的天气。在大气层的高处，这些灰烬把日光从我们这个星球反射出去。最后，逐渐使地球上的温度降低了。

---

fertile *adj.* 肥沃的  　　　　　　　　　　　　　　barren *adj.* 贫瘠的
visible *adj.* 明显的；看得见的

♦ A VOLCANO WAKES UP

For the Zoque Indians, the effect was direct and *devastating*. The volcano destroyed their homes and villages. It wiped out their farms. And it killed entire families. The exact number of dead will never be known. The whole thing happened in a remote part of Mexico. Birth records were not always up-to-date. And, *in any case*, the ash and rocks buried people whose bodies will never be found.

The official count was 187 dead. But no one believes that. The real figure is likely in the thousands. The World Almanac puts the number of dead at 1,880. Whatever the number, this was a major disaster for the people of the region.

Now, of course, scientists are taking El Chichón more seriously. These days, it is considered to be a young, active volcano. Experts believe that it will erupt again. And this time it may not take thousands of years to do so.

---

对于索克印第安人来说，它的影响是直接的和毁灭性的。火山爆发破坏了他们的家园和村庄，毁灭了整个家庭。确切的死亡数字不可能统计出来了。这一切发生在墨西哥偏远地区，人口出生记录总是不能及时更新。并且，无论如何，被火山灰和熔岩掩埋的人们的尸体是无法被发现的。

官方的统计数字是187人死亡，但是没有人相信它。真正的数字很可能是几千人。世界年鉴把死亡数字定在1880人。不论具体数字是多少，对这一地区的人们来说，这是一场巨大的灾难。

当然，现在，科学家已经更严肃地对待埃尔奇琼火山了。现在，科学家们认为它是一座年轻的活火山。专家们相信它会再次爆发。这一次，恐怕不会用上几千年的时间了。

---

devastating  adj.  毁灭性的                    in any case  无论如何

## TOTAL PANIC

# 16

# Death Rides the Subway

Six million people took the Tokyo subway each day. It was an easy, comfortable ride. People could grab a nap on the way to work or school. The *subway* was clean—so clean that the workers who ran it wore white gloves. And it was safe. There were no gangs *roaming* the cars

*On March 20, 1995, a mysterious gas spread through the Tokyo subway system. Only the luckiest riders were able to stagger out. Twelve subway patrons died, and 5,500 more needed medical attention. Even during the cleanup, workers had to wear gas masks. Who was to blame for this disaster?*

---

## 地铁死亡之旅

1995年3月20日，一种神秘的气体在东京的地铁系统里扩散开来。只有一名乘客能够侥幸从地铁里跌跌撞撞地逃出来。12名乘客死亡，5500人需要医疗救助。甚至在清理现场时，工作人员还是需要戴上防毒面具。谁该为这场灾难负责呢？

每天东京有600万人乘坐地铁。乘坐地铁是方便而又舒适的。在上班或去学校的路上，人们能够小憩片刻。地铁是清洁的——它是如此清洁，以至于驾驶员都戴着白手套。它又是安全的，没有那些在汽车里到处游荡

---

subway  *n.*  地铁                              roam  *v.*  闲逛；漫步

◆ DEATH RIDES THE SUBWAY

looking for trouble. Quiet, clean, and safe—the Tokyo subway stood as a symbol of modern Japan.

That image *vanished* on March 20, 1995. During the morning rush hour, terrorists struck. They planted a nerve gas called sarin on the subway. Sarin is extremely *lethal* in both its liquid and vapor forms. Less than one drop can easily kill a human. Sarin was invented in Germany in the 1930s. The Nazis used it in their death camps. Sarin attacks the lungs, causing people to *suffocate*. In minutes, its victims are dead.

That was what Tokyo's *commuters* were up against. Death was riding the subway that morning. But no one knew it. Probably only a handful of people had even heard of sarin. There was no reason to think it would ever show up in a subway.

---

找麻烦的人。安静，清洁，安全——东京地铁成为现代日本的一个象征。

这种景象在1995年3月20日突然消失了。在上午交通的高峰时段，恐怖分子出手了，他们把一种叫作沙林的神经毒气放置在地铁中。沙林处于气态和液态时都是致命的，不到一滴的剂量就可以轻易毒死一个人。沙林是德国人19世纪30年代发明的，纳粹分子把它用在了他们的死亡营里。沙林会侵袭肺部，引起窒息。几分钟内，受害人就会死亡。

这就是东京那些通勤一族面临的情况。那天上午，死神就坐在地铁车厢里面。但是没有人知道这个情况，甚至可能只有少数人听说过沙林。人们没有理由想到它竟然会出现在地铁中。

---

vanish *v.* 消失
suffocate *v.* 窒息

lethal *adj.* 致命的
commuter *n.* 通勤者

### TOTAL PANIC

The terrorists used lunch boxes and soft drink bottles to sneak the sarin into the subway. They left these items in trains on three different lines. The gas leaked out just as the three trains *converged* on the central station. Tokyo's police headquarters was just outside the station. Officials later said the terrorists had two goals. One was to kill as many people as possible. The other was to thumb their noses at the police.

Kasumasa Takahashi worked on the subway. His post was at the central station. A little after eight o'clock, a train pulled in. Takahashi noticed something strange. People began spilling out of the first car in pain. Some had tears rolling down their cheeks. Others were *foaming* at the mouth. "What's wrong?" cried Takahashi.

He ran over to the car. There he saw a small package wrapped

---

恐怖分子用饭盒和饮料瓶把沙林暗中带入地铁。并把这些包装好的毒剂分散在三条不同线路的列车中，就在三辆列车汇合在中心车站那一刻，毒气开始向外泄漏。东京警察总署就在这个车站外面。事后警官们说，恐怖分子有两个目的。一是杀死尽可能多的人，另一个是向警方示威。

高桥正在地铁里工作，他的岗位就在中心地铁站。八点刚过，一趟列车进站了。高桥注意到出现了一些奇怪的情况。人们开始痛苦不堪地走出第一节车厢。有些人顺着脸颊流下了眼泪，还有人口吐白沫。高桥喊道："怎么回事？"

高桥跑进车厢。在那里，他看见用报纸包着的一个小包裹。高桥把它

---

converge  *v.*  聚合     foam  *v.*  吐白沫；起泡沫

◆ DEATH RIDES THE SUBWAY

in newspaper. Takahashi picked it up and carried it away. As he went, drops of liquid fell on the platform tiles. It looked like nothing more than water. So he stopped to wipe them up. As he bent over, he blacked out and *collapsed*. Takahashi died later that day in the hospital.

One woman was on her way to work. She got off a train at the central station. As she did so, she noticed a *weird* smell. "The smell was something I had never experienced," she said. She put a handkerchief over her mouth and began climbing the stairs to get out of the subway. Her head started to *pound*. Her vision became *blurry*. With each step she grew sicker and sicker. She had to fight back the urge to throw up. "When I got outside, I crouched down," she recalled. "So many people were like me, crouched on the ground."

---

捡起来拿了出去。他正走着，几滴液体掉到了站台的瓷砖上，看上去和水珠一样。所以他停下脚步，想擦去这些液滴。正当弯腰的时候，他突然眼前一黑，摔倒在地。当天晚些时候，高桥死在医院里。

　　一位妇人正在上班的路上。在中心车站，她走下一趟列车。这时，她闻到了一种奇怪的气味。她说："这种气味我从来没闻过。"她把一块手帕放在嘴上，开始上楼梯，准备出地铁站。她突然觉得头晕眼花，每走一步，她都越来越难受。她强忍着没有呕吐。她后来回忆道："当我走出去的时候，我缩着身子蹲了下去。那么多人都和我一样，缩着身子蹲在地上。"

---

collapse  *v.*  倒塌　　　　　　　　　　　　　weird  *adj.*  怪异的
pound  *v.*  连续地猛击或猛撞某物　　　　　　blurry  *adj.*  模糊的

### TOTAL PANIC

This woman was one of thousands injured in the attack. They all stumbled out or were carried out of the subway gasping for fresh air. Many were bleeding from the nose and *vomiting*.

One victim didn't feel bad at first. But as he headed for his office, he began to feel funny. "The sunlight suddenly seemed to brighten. My vision got *hazy*," he said. "I felt my chest being pressed, and my neck became *stiff*. I had a headache."

Twelve people died from their exposure to sarin that morning. More than 5,500 others were injured. The *terrorists* had shattered the city's sense of safety. They had planted fear in the hearts of the Japanese people. In the days that followed the attack, many of them refused to ride the subway. It was no longer a safe place to be.

---

这位妇人是这次袭击事件几千名受害者之一。他们都步履艰难地，甚至是被搀扶着走出地铁站，大口呼吸着新鲜空气，很多人鼻孔出血，连连呕吐。

有一名受害者起初并没有感到不适。当时正当他走向办公室的时候，他开始有一种奇异的感觉。他说："阳光好像突然变亮了。我的眼前开始模糊不清。我觉得胸口好像被什么压着，脖子变硬了。我开始头疼。"

那个上午，共有12人在沙林泄漏中死亡，超过5500人受伤。恐怖分子粉碎了这座城市中的安全感。他们在日本人的心灵里埋下深深的恐惧感。袭击事件发生后的一段时间里，很多人拒绝乘坐地铁，那里不再是一个安全的地方了。

---

vomit *v.* 呕吐  
stiff *adj.* 僵硬的  

hazy *adj.* 模糊的  
terrorist *n.* 恐怖分子

◆ DEATH RIDES THE SUBWAY

Newspapers around the world *condemned* the attack. One Japanese paper called it "mass murder" and "an unthinkable crime." A U.S. paper described it as "ghastly." An Israeli paper called the terrorists "mindless criminals."

Who were these terrorists? In most cases, the guilty *parties* come forward to accept the blame. That's why they commit their crimes in the first place. Terrorists want people to pay attention to them. But this time no one stepped forward.

Still, the police had a pretty good idea who was behind the attack. They suspected it was a man named Shoko Asahara. He was the head of a *religious* sect known as the "Supreme Truth." Asahara was arrested. In his house, the police found materials needed to make sarin. They also found millions of dollars in *cash* and gold. The

全世界的报纸都谴责了这次袭击事件。一份日本报纸称其为"一场大规模的谋杀"和"不可思议的罪行"。一家美国报纸称这个事件是"恐怖的"。一家以色列报纸称恐怖分子为"没有头脑的罪犯"。

这些恐怖分子是谁呢？在多数情况下，当事人都会自愿接受谴责。这就是他们首先承认罪行的原因。恐怖分子想让人们注意到他们的存在，但是这一次，没有一个人站出来。

尽管如此，警方还是很清楚地知道这次袭击的幕后指使者是谁。他们怀疑这是一名叫作麻原彰晃的男子。他是一个名为"奥姆真理教"的宗教组织的头目。麻原被捕了。在他的房间里，警方发现了制作沙林所需要的原料，还发现了数百万现金以及黄金。警方随即指控是麻原主使了这次袭击事件。

condemn *v.* 谴责
religious *adj.* 宗教的
party *n.* 当事人
cash *n.* 现金

## TOTAL PANIC

police then charged Asahara with *masterminding* the attack.

Why would Asahara commit such an awful crime? It isn't clear. But he had certainly developed a twisted view of himself and of the world. For example, Asahara seemed to believe he could fly. He didn't need a plane, he said. He could do it all by himself. At one point, he claimed that he could stay *aloft* for three seconds. Even better days lay ahead. "Within a year," he predicted, "my body should be able to fly at will."

That wasn't his only strange *boast*. Asahara said that he could read people's minds. He claimed he could see into the future. And, like Superman, he said he had X-ray vision. All these skills he promised to teach his followers. Surprisingly, many people believed him. Asahara had 10,000 followers in Japan. He had 20,000 more in the rest of the world. These people were true believers. They turned

---

麻原为什么会犯下这么让人恐怖的罪行呢？现在还不清楚，但他肯定有了对他自己以及整个世界的一种极度扭曲的观点。例如，麻原似乎相信他能够飞行。他说不需要飞机，自己就能做到，还宣称自己能在空中停留3秒钟。更有甚者，这种本领还能加强。他预言道："一年之内，我就能随心所欲地飞行了。"

这还不是他唯一自以为是的地方。麻原说他能够看出别人的意念。他宣称自己能够预见未来，并且，他说自己和超人一样，能够用X射线看东西。他承诺会把所有这些技能传授给追随者。令人奇怪的是，很多人都相信他说的话。在日本，麻原有10,000名追随者，在世界各地，他还有其他20,000名追随者，这些人是虔诚的信徒。他们把所有的钱都交给麻原，每

---

mastermind *v.* 策划      aloft *adv.* 在空中
boast *n.* 自夸；自吹自擂

◆ DEATH RIDES THE SUBWAY

over all their money to him. And each time they met him, they kissed his big toe.

Such nonsense was pretty harmless. But there was a much darker side to Asahara. He declared that the last world war would begin in 1997. The *primary* weapon, he predicted, would be sarin. He told his followers to get ready for the coming battle. He told them they should welcome death.

One expert on terrorism explained that it is tough to deal with *lunatics* like Asahara. How do you fight someone, he asked "whose idea of a happy death is mass suicide?"

There was no easy answer for that. Toyko's commuters did slowly return to the subway. But fear continued to hang in the air. People now realized that terrorists could strike anywhere, even on a "safe" subway train in Japan.

---

次见他的时候，他们都会亲吻他的大脚趾。

　　这些荒谬的说法本身是没有什么害处的。但是麻原还有一个更为阴暗的侧面。他宣称最后一次世界大战将在1997年打响。他预言，首选的武器就是沙林。他告诉追随者为这场即将到来的战争做好准备。他告诉他们，应该坦然面对死神。

　　一位研究恐怖主义的专家解释说，对待类似麻原这样的疯子是非常艰苦的。如何跟这种人做斗争？专家说："谁会认为有一种快乐的死法，那就是集体自杀呢？"

　　对这个问题，没有一个很轻松的答案。东京的通勤一族慢慢回到地铁中。但是恐慌情绪继续笼罩在空中。现在人们意识到，恐怖分子可能在任何地方发动袭击，甚至是在东京"安全的"地铁车厢里也不例外。

---

primary　*adj.*　首要的　　　　　　　　　　　lunatic　*n.*　疯子

TOTAL PANIC

# 17

# Hit by a Bullet

On July 2, 1994, life was looking pretty good for Kim Williams. She was playing the best *golf* of her life. Her drives were long and straight. Her chips and putts were right on the mark. For once, she felt as if she could *beat* anyone.

This was quite a change for

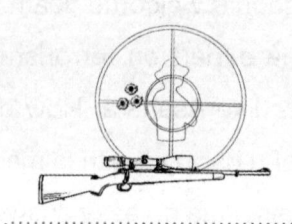

*Shortly after being shot in the neck by a hunter's stray bullet, Williams returned to the golf course to play one of the best games of her career.*

---

# 被子弹击中

在威廉姆斯的颈部被猎人的飞弹误伤后没有多久,她就重返高尔夫球赛场,打出了她事业中最好的一场。

1994年7月2日对金·威廉姆斯来说是很不错的一天。这是她一生中高尔夫球打得最好的一天。她的击球远而且走直线,低球和短打都很准。她曾经一度认为可以击败任何人。

这对于威廉姆斯来说是一个很大的转变。以前她都没有这么幸运。

---

golf   n.   高尔夫球       beat   v.   打败;击败

◆ HIT BY A BULLET

Williams. Until this point she had not had much luck. In six years as a *professional* golfer, she had struggled. Her total winnings were just $23,077. Williams had not won a single tournament. In fact, she had never come close. It was now halfway through the 1994 season. Again, she had started the year poorly. She had failed to finish among the top 20 golfers in her first 14 *tournaments*.

But at the Youngstown-Warren Classic she turned her game around. Things looked better—much better. The Classic is a three-day, 54-hole tournament. Williams had a great first day. On the second day it rained. The women had to stop playing after just 10 holes. But at last Williams was up with the leaders. She was just two strokes behind. She felt poised to win for the first time. Better yet, she was on the *verge* of cashing her first big paycheck.

---

作为一名职业高尔夫球运动员，在六年的运动生涯中她赢得的全部奖金只有23,077美元。她没有在任何一场联赛中取得冠军。实际上她从来就没有接近过这个层次。现在1994赛季已经过半。今年也一样，开局还是不顺利。从她开始打的14场联赛来看，她没有进前20强。

但是在扬斯敦—沃伦古典赛中她的情况发生了巨大的转变。情形看起来变得好了起来——应该说是好多了。这场古典赛是连续3天，打54洞的联赛。威廉姆斯第一天打得非常好。第二天开始下雨。女子运动员们打完了10个洞后只好暂停。但是威廉姆斯的成绩已经接近了领先的运动员，她仅仅落后两击。她觉得能取得冠军应该不是个意外。这次打得很好，她已经触到了大奖的边了。

---

professional *adj.* 职业的；专业的  tournament *n.* 锦标赛；联赛
verge *n.* 边缘

### TOTAL PANIC

That night, Williams headed to a *drugstore*. She needed some baby oil. She used the oil on her *putter*. The oil kept the club from getting rusty when it rained.

As Williams walked toward the store entrance, she suddenly felt a sharp pain in the left side of her neck. "It felt like somebody hit a baseball line drive into me," she later said.

"What was that?" she asked herself.

For a split second, she thought it might have been a golf ball. But she wasn't on a golf course. She was standing on a sidewalk next to a parking lot. "Then I put my hand up to my neck and pulled it down," she said. "It was covered with blood." Only then did she realize what had happened. She had been shot!

Williams walked into the drugstore. She was still *in a daze* and

---

那天晚上，威廉姆斯步行到一家药店。她需要买一些婴儿油。她把油涂在轻击球杆上，这样在下雨时可以防止生锈。

当威廉姆斯走到药店的入口处时，她突然感到颈部的左边一阵钻心的疼痛。"我感觉就好像是有人抛出的一记大力垒球发球击中了我，"她后来说。

"怎么回事？"她想。

一瞬间，她又想到可能是一个高尔夫球。但是她没有站在高尔夫球场中。她现在站在停车场旁边的人行道上。"我用手抓了一下脖子，然后伸开手，"她说，"上面全是血。"这时她才意识到出事了，她被子弹击中了！

威廉姆斯走进药店。她觉得一阵晕眩，不知道该怎么办。她请人拨打

---

drugstore  n. 药店
in a daze  迷茫；茫然

putter  n. 轻击球杆

◆ HIT BY A BULLET

not quite sure what to do. She asked someone to call 911. Then she *slumped* to the floor. A man grabbed some paper towels. Pressing them to Williams's neck, he tried to stop the bleeding.

"Oh my God, I'm going to bleed to death!" she remembered thinking.

A few minutes later, an *ambulance* arrived. Williams was rushed to the hospital. The police also hurried to the *scene*. They had lots of questions but few answers. Where had the shot come from? Who had fired it? Why would anyone want to shoot Williams?

At first, it seemed that Kim Williams might have been the victim of a drive-by shooting. In other words, someone might have driven by and shot at her from a car window. But the next day the police learned the truth. The shooting had been a *bizarre* accident. A man

---

911，然后就跌倒在地上。一个人把一些纸巾压在她的伤口上，试图为她止血。

"啊，天哪！我这样流血会死的！"她记得当时的想法。

几分钟后一辆救护车来了。威廉姆斯被用最快的速度送到了医院。警察也用最快的速度赶到了现场。他们有很多的疑问，但是几乎没有答案。子弹是从哪里射来的呢？谁开的枪？射向威廉姆斯干什么？

刚开始，看起来好像是一起驱车射击事件。也就是说，有人开车经过，从车窗中向威廉姆斯开枪。但是第二天警方才得知事情的真相。这次

---

slump *v.* 重重地坐下（或倒下）
scene *n.* 事发地点

ambulance *n.* 救护车
bizarre *adj.* 奇异的

**TOTAL PANIC**

from a nearby township *confessed* to the crime. He had been taking target practice in the woods about a mile away. One of his bullets missed the *target*. It flew out of the woods and struck Kim Williams in the neck.

When Williams arrived at the hospital, doctors quickly went to work on her. They discovered that the bullet was lodged against her *esophagus*. Yet they couldn't believe how lucky she was. The bullet hadn't hit any organs. The doctors took several tests. At last, they decided not to take the bullet out. It was too risky. The operation might do more harm than good. Instead, they decided to wait and see how she healed with the bullet still inside her.

For the next several hours, Williams drifted in and out of sleep. At first she was listed in only "fair" condition, but she grew more *stable*

---

枪击事件是一次古怪的事故。附近小镇的一个人承认与此有关。他在大约一英里外的树林里打靶。其中有一枪没有击中靶子，就是这颗子弹飞出了树林击中了威廉姆斯的脖子。

威廉姆斯被送到医院，医生们马上开始为她治疗。他们发现子弹紧贴着食道。他们几乎难以置信，她太幸运了，子弹没有击中任何器官。医生们尝试了好几次，最后他们决定不把子弹取出。取出太冒险了，手术的害处多于好处。相反他们决定等等看她的愈合情况。

其后的几个小时，威廉姆斯时睡时醒。开始她被列为"普通"医护级别，但是她的状况越来越稳定。一名护士进来看了看她的监控表，结果表

---

confess  *v.*  承认                          target  *n.*  目标
esophagus  *n.*  食管；食道                  stable  *adj.*  稳定的

◆ HIT BY A BULLET

with each passing minute. At one point a nurse came in and looked at Williams's *chart*. It showed that Williams was getting better much faster than anyone expected. "Wow!" the nurse exclaimed. "You had an angel on your shoulder."

Williams agreed. Later she said she could feel the bullet every time she *swallowed*. But at least she was alive. "I feel lucky," she said. "There's really no explanation for it. It's a miracle that a bullet can go through your neck and not hit anything."

After just two days in the hospital, Williams was released. She had a bright red scar on her neck. It hurt to move her head. Her legs felt weak. Still, she wanted to get right back out and start playing golf again. She had missed the end of the Youngstown-Warren Classic. But another tournament was coming up the following

---

明威廉姆斯恢复得比预想的要快。"哦！你真幸运。"护士很高兴地说。

威廉姆斯同意这种看法。后来她说，当她吞咽的时候，她能感到子弹的存在，但至少她还活着。"我觉得幸运，这简直太不可思议了，子弹穿过颈部而没有伤到任何器官。"她说。

威廉姆斯在医院只住了两天就出院了。她的颈部有个浅色的红伤疤。当她头部移动时，会感到疼痛。她感到腿很软。但是她还是想马上回到高尔夫球赛场。她已经错过了扬斯敦—沃伦古典赛的最后比赛。但是这一周

---

chart *n.* 图；图表　　　　　　　　　　　swallow *v.* 吞咽

TOTAL PANIC

weekend. It was called the Jamie Farr Toledo Classic. To everyone's surprise, Williams entered it.

Williams wasn't sure she would have the strength to make it around the course. But somehow she did. In the first round, she shot an 18-hole score of 68. That tied her best score for the year. She was so tired at the end of the round that she nearly collapsed. She had to be driven to the first-aid tent for *fluids* and rest. She said her *fatigue* was "frightening." Her legs felt "like Jell-O." Nonetheless, she didn't drop out.

Williams went on to play the last two rounds. Again, she did very well. She shot a 72 followed by a 70. That was good enough to tie for 10th place. It was her best finish of the year. She won almost $10,000 in the tournament.

---

　　的周末还有一场联赛，是吉米·法尔·托勒多古典赛。令人吃惊的是，威廉姆斯参加了这场比赛。
　　威廉姆斯也不知道她能否坚持下来。但是她还是坚持了下来。在第一场中18洞，她得了68分，是她一年中最好的成绩。这一场结束后她感到非常疲劳，几乎要倒下了。她被送到急救帐篷输液和休息。她说她的疲劳是"很可怕的"。她觉得她的腿"就好像果冻一样无力"。但无论如何，她都没有放弃。
　　威廉姆斯继续打了另外两场。这两场她也打得很好。分别得了72分和70分。这可以得到第十名的成绩，是她一年中的最好成绩。这次联赛中她获得了10,000美元的奖金。

---

fluid　*n.*　流体；液体　　　　　　　　　　　　　　　　　fatigue　*n.*　疲劳

◆ HIT BY A BULLET

Williams found that the accident had made her famous. Several different news organizations wanted to report her story. People who had never heard of her before now called her by name. As one friend said, "At least everyone knows you're Kim Williams now."

Williams even found she could joke a bit about the shooting. "I don't mean to make fun," she later said, "but I might *endorse* Target Drug Stores." Or perhaps she could endorse Bullet golf clubs. She could give new meaning to their *slogan*, "No. 1 with a bullet."

---

威廉姆斯发现这场事故使她出了名。好几家媒体打算报道她的故事。以前根本没有关注过她的人开始叫她的名字。像一个朋友所说的："现在，最终所有的人都知道你就是金·威廉姆斯了。"

威廉姆斯甚至发现她可以就这次射击事件开开玩笑。后来她说："我是当真的，我签名可以是'药店的靶子'。"或者她可以签"子弹高尔夫球俱乐部"。她可以给这个俱乐部带来全新的标语："带着子弹的第一名"。

---

endorse  *v.*  签名                    slogan  *n.*  标语

# TOTAL PANIC

## 18

# Trapped on the 37th Floor

Melinda Skaar wasn't expecting any phone calls. Skaar was working late in her office at the First *Interstate* Bank of California. By 10:45 that night—May 4, 1988—she was almost ready to go home. That's when the phone rang.

Picking it up, she heard a *security*

*The 1988 fire in the First Interstate Bank building was the worst high-rise fire in Los Angeles's history.*

---

## 高楼遇困

1988年在第一州际银行大厦发生的火灾是洛杉矶历史上最严重的高层大火。

米林达·斯卡尔没有想到会有电话。斯卡尔在加利福尼亚第一州际银行的办公室加晚班。当时是1988年5月4日大约晚上10:45，她正打算回家，电话响了。

她拿起了话机，听到电话另一头的保卫人员喊到："失火了！马上离

---

interstate  *adj.*  州际的                    security  *n.*  保安

◆ TRAPPED ON THE 37TH FLOOR

guard on the other end of the line. "There's a fire!" he shouted. "Get out of there!"

Skaar didn't *panic*. She figured that it was just a small *blaze* elsewhere in the building. Her office building was huge. There were 62 floors in the First Interstate Tower. Skaar's desk was on the 37th floor. Skaar called out to office mate Stephen Oksas, who had also stayed late to work. The two of them headed for the hallway. But when they got there, they were met by a cloud of black smoke. They rushed back into the main office. Slamming the door, Skaar took off her jacket. She *stuffed* it into the crack at the bottom of the door. She hoped that would keep the smoke from seeping in.

Then she and Oksas turned to the phone. They called 911 and reported that they were trapped. Before they could call their families,

---

开！"

斯卡尔没有惊慌，她觉得就是这栋楼里面哪个小地方失火了。她的办公楼很大，第一州际大厦里面有62层。斯卡尔的办公室在第三十七层。斯卡尔马上叫上同事史蒂芬·奥萨斯，他也在办公室里面加班。他们俩向楼梯走去，但是当他们到达那里时发现一片黑色的浓烟。他们马上冲回大办公室，关上门，斯卡尔脱下外衣，把它塞到门下面的缝隙中。希望能够把烟雾挡在外面。

然后他们拨通了911，说他们被困住了。他们刚想给家里打个电话，

---

panic *v.* 惊慌  
stuff *v.* 填塞；塞满

blaze *n.* 火焰

**TOTAL PANIC**

however, the line went dead. That meant that they were completely cut off from the outside world. All they could do was to wait and hope someone would come to rescue them.

Skaar and Oksas didn't know it, but they were caught in the worst high-rise fire in Los Angeles's history. The blaze began on the 12th floor. From there, it spread quickly to the next four levels. Temperatures on those floors rose to 2,000 degrees. The air was so hot that it melted metal. It blew out windows. It also melted the glue that held the *carpets* in place. The burning glue filled the air with black, *toxic* fumes.

The giant blaze could be seen for miles around. Three hundred *firefighters* were called in. Most had never seen anything like it before. They struggled bravely, but the fire kept spreading.

---

线路就切断了。这意味着他们完全与外界切断了。他们所能做的就是呆在那里，等待救援。

斯卡尔和奥萨斯并不知道他们被洛杉矶历史上最大的一场高层大火围困住了。大火是从第十二层燃起的。火势很快就蔓延到了相邻的4层，那些层的温度达到了2000度。空气的温度是如此之高，以至于把金属都融化了。火烧掉了窗户，融化了固定地毯的胶带。这些烧着的胶产生了大量的有毒气体。

这场大火在几英里外都能看得到。大约有三百名消防队员来到了现场。大多数人根本就没有见过这种阵势。他们勇敢地进行着扑救，但是火

---

carpet *n.* 地毯　　　　　　　　　　　　toxic *adj.* 有毒的；中毒的
firefighter *n.* 消防人员

◆ TRAPPED ON THE 37TH FLOOR

Firefighters knew that if it got past the 16th floor, the whole building might collapse.

Meanwhile, up on the 37th floor, Skaar and Oksas waited. The minutes ticked by. Smoke began to *waft* into the office. It billowed up the stairwells and through the air vents. Soon it became hard for Skaar and Oksas to breathe.

They thought about trying to run down the 37 flights of stairs. Or they could head up the remaining flights to the roof. But they didn't think they could make it. They would probably die from smoke *inhalation* before they even got close to safety.

Looking around, they spotted a small workroom. It seemed to have cleaner air. So Skaar and Oksas *huddled* in there. "We found these ... water bottles in there and cut holes in the bottom," Skaar later recalled. "Then we put paper towels over the holes to filter the

---

势还在蔓延。消防队员们知道如果大火一直向上蔓延过16层，整座大楼可能倒塌。

当时，斯卡尔和奥萨斯正在37层等待。时间正在流逝，烟雾开始钻进办公室。烟雾冲进楼梯间，钻进气孔里。很快，斯卡尔和奥萨斯开始觉得呼吸困难。

他们考虑跑下37层的楼梯。或者他们一直向上跑，跑到楼顶。但是他们又觉得不可行。可能他们没有到达安全地点就被烟雾熏死了。

他们仔细看看周围，又发现一个小工作间，好像里面的空气清新些。斯卡尔和奥萨斯就挤在里面。"我们在里面发现了一些水瓶，就在下面切

---

waft *v.* 飘荡
inhalation *n.* 吸入

huddle *v.* 挤在一起

## TOTAL PANIC

air and we breathed through those."

That helped for a while, but in time even the workroom was filled with deadly smoke. The bottles weren't much good then. Skaar and Oksas did everything they could to find fresh air. They went to a cupboard in the corner of the room. Every once in a while they opened the door. They took a deep breath of clean air and then quickly closed the door again.

Oksas and Skaar knew they were running out of time. *Desperate*, they tried to break one of the outside windows, but the glass was not breakable. It was sealed with a heavy rubber coating. Oksas picked up a table. He threw it at a window. It just bounced back. Together, he and Skaar picked up an empty file *cabinet*. They *flung* it at the window. It, too, bounced to the floor. They tried other windows, but the same thing happened. They picked up other cabinets and

---

了洞，"斯卡尔后来回忆道，"然后我们把纸巾盖在洞的上面，用它过滤空气，从里面呼吸。"

这起了一会儿的作用，但是不一会儿，这个小工作间里面也充满了致命的烟雾。瓶子也没有作用了。斯卡尔和奥萨斯竭尽所能来寻找新鲜空气。他们来到房间角落的一个墙柜跟前，打开门，一齐吸一口新鲜空气，然后马上关上柜门。

奥萨斯和斯卡尔知道他们的时间不多了。他们打算做最后一搏，试图打碎外层的玻璃，但是那层玻璃却十分坚固，上面被一层厚橡胶封得严严实实。奥萨斯举起了桌子，扔向窗户，它弹了回来。他和斯卡尔一起把空文件箱举了起来，砸向窗户，还是弹了回来。他们挨个窗户试，可是效果

---

desperate *adj.* 绝望的  
fling *v.* 挥动

cabinet *n.* 箱；柜

◆ TRAPPED ON THE 37TH FLOOR

threw those. "They just *bounced* back," said Skaar. "Everything just bounced back."

At last, Skaar grabbed a pair of scissors. She tried to *scrape* away the rubber coating at the edge of the window. She worked and worked. She managed to let in a tiny hair-thin trickle of air. That was it. It didn't provide enough oxygen for even a single breath.

Defeated, Skaar and Oksas *staggered* back to the workroom. They felt weak and dizzy. Shortly after that, Skaar heard a helicopter outside. "I thought I had to wave to them, to let them know we were still alive," she said. So she left Oksas and stumbled back out to the main room. She waved at the helicopter, but she didn't have much hope. She didn't think rescuers could ever reach her in time.

"I thought, I'm definitely [going] to die in this," she said. "I thought about all the things that would go unfinished in my life. How people

---

一样。他们又抬起其他柜子去砸还是一样。"又弹回来了，所有的东西都弹回来了。"

最后斯卡尔拿起了一把剪子。她尽力把玻璃边上的橡胶划开。她使尽全力，终于开了一点小口，有一小缕的空气吹了进来，但是连吸一口都不够。

斯卡尔和奥萨斯失败了，他们又冲回了小工作间。他们觉得很虚弱，头晕眼花。很快，斯卡尔听到一阵直升飞机的声音。"我觉得我们要向它挥手，让他们知道我们还活着，"她说。所以她离开奥萨斯跌跌撞撞地来到大办公室。她向直升机挥手，但是她没有抱太大的希望，甚至觉得救援人员不能按时进来。

"我觉得我是死定了，"她说，"我想到我这一生所有没完成的事

---

bounce *v.* 弹起；弹回　　　　　　　　　　　scrape *v.* 刮
stagger *v.* 蹒跚

**TOTAL PANIC**

would find us, here, on the floor...I thought about my parents, about my family ..."

After she felt her way back to the workroom, she found that Oksas had passed out. Skaar knew she couldn't hang on much longer, either. By this time, she could barely walk. She *shuffled* over to the window where the tiny trickle of air was *drifting* in. Then she, too, collapsed.

As Skaar and Oksas lay near death, rescuers were rushing to find them. It had taken three and a half hours, but firefighters had finally brought the fire under control. By 2:15 A.M. they had beaten it back. Soon after, they found the body of one man who had died in an elevator. They rescued several people from the roof and one man from the 50th floor. The only ones left to be found were Skaar and

---

业。人们如何找到我们，在这里，在地板上……我想到我的父母，我的家庭……"

当她摸回工作间时，她发现奥萨斯已经昏过去了。斯卡尔知道她也坚持不了多长时间。这时她也几乎不能走动了。她扑到窗户那一丝空气的地方。然后她也昏了过去。

当斯卡尔和奥萨斯躺在地上失去知觉时，救援人员冲了进来搜索他们。已经过去了三个半小时，最终人们控制住了火势。到凌晨2:15时，他们把火控制得差不多了。很快，人们发现在电梯里有一个人的尸体。他们在楼顶上救了几个人，50楼救了一个人，最后搜索到的就是斯卡尔和奥萨斯。

---

shuffle  *v.*  拖着脚走             drift  *v.*  漂移；漂流

◆ TRAPPED ON THE 37TH FLOOR

Oksas.

At last, at about 4 A.M., firefighters reached the 37th floor. There they saw Oksas and Skaar. "All I remember is seeing these bodies …" said Skaar. "Strong bodies that weren't like ours, bodies that could walk and breathe and had equipment with them and would rescue us."

The firefighters pulled *curtains* off the windows and used them as *stretchers*. Then they hurried Skaar and Oksas outside. Both were rushed to the hospital.

Melinda Skaar and Stephen Oksas knew they were lucky to be alive. "Sunday's my birthday," Skaar told one reporter the next day. She would be turning 29. But she knew that she had already gotten the best present possible—the gift of life.

---

最后，在大约凌晨四点的时候，消防队员到达了37楼。他们发现了斯卡尔和奥萨斯。"我只记得看到了那些人……" 斯卡尔说，"不像我们，而是很强壮的身体，他们能走，能呼吸，带着装备，能够援救我们。"

消防队员把房间窗户上的窗帘扯了下来，做成简易担架，把斯卡尔和奥萨斯运了出来，然后马上送到了医院。

米林达·斯卡尔和史蒂芬·奥萨斯知道他们太幸运了。"星期日是我的生日，"第二天斯卡尔告诉记者。她将29岁了。但是她知道她得到了最好的礼物——生命。

---

curtain  *n.*  窗帘          stretcher  *n.*  担架